THE SCORE

THE
SCORE

The Ultimate Quiz
to Test Who He Is

Allison Castillo

A PERIGEE BOOK

THE BERKLEY PUBLISHING GROUP
Published by the Penguin Group
Penguin Group (USA) Inc.
375 Hudson Street, New York, New York 10014, USA
Penguin Group (Canada), 90 Eglinton Avenue East, Suite 700, Toronto, Ontario M4P
2Y3, Canada (a division of Pearson Penguin Canada Inc.)
Penguin Books Ltd., 80 Strand, London WC2R 0RL, England
Penguin Group Ireland, 25 St. Stephen's Green, Dublin 2, Ireland (a division of Penguin
Books Ltd.)
Penguin Group (Australia), 250 Camberwell Road, Camberwell, Victoria 3124, Australia
(a division of Pearson Australia Group Pty. Ltd.)
Penguin Books India Pvt. Ltd., 11 Community Centre, Panchsheel Park, New Delhi—
110 017, India
Penguin Group (NZ), cnr. Airborne and Rosedale Roads, Albany, Auckland 1310, New
Zealand (a division of Pearson New Zealand Ltd.)
Penguin Books (South Africa) (Pty.) Ltd., 24 Sturdee Avenue, Rosebank, Johannesburg
2196, South Africa
Penguin Books Ltd., Registered Offices: 80 Strand, London WC2R 0RL, England

ISBN: 0-399-53247-1

PRINTING HISTORY
Perigee trade paperback edition / January 2006

PERIGEE is a registered trademark of Penguin Group (USA) Inc.
The "P" design is a trademark belonging to Penguin Group (USA) Inc.

This book has been cataloged by the Library of Congress

PRINTED IN THE UNITED STATES OF AMERICA

10 9 8 7 6 5 4 3 2 1

This one's for the ladies.

ACKNOWLEDGMENTS

Thanks to Patrick Nolan at Penguin for thinking my years of failed relationships could finally be put to good use. Thanks to my editor at Perigee, Michelle Howry, for being a pleasure to work with, a super talent and having a great sense of humor. Thanks to Christel Winkler at Perigee for jumping in with such enthusiasm at the eleventh hour. Thanks to my agent, Paula Balzer, for her guidance and advice.

Many women contributed to this book in various ways, from sharing unique and entertaining stories and opinions, to sharing generous support and encouragement. Heartfelt thanks goes out to Ciara Breslin, Mary Donnelly, Jen Kirkman, Joanna Lehan, Kathleen McAree, Megan Tropea, Maggie Powers, Padma Atluri, Nicole Smith, Eileen Rivard, Cindy Tenner, Edith Meyer, Ellen Schultz, Kristen Ardigo, Rena Zager, Lynn Harris, Lisa Nicoll, Stacie Davis, Sharyn Wolf,

Lauren Graham, Kathy Ebel, Elise Nersesian, Laurel Haines, Lauren Young, Diana Katz, Karen Fox, Claire Schaper and Melissa Walker. Here's to The Ladies Who Brunch! aka Amanda Melson, Sue Prekel, Deb Rabbai, and Maria Sharpe. I cannot thank you enough for your time, much needed input, and love of Bloody Marys. Thanks, Abby Scott, for being a math whiz!

Thanks to the fellas who helped and hopefully continue to speak to me: Bryan Olsen, Benari Poulten (happy?), Baron Vaughn, Bob Powers, Greg Ainsworth, Eric Deskin, Doug Fields, Dan Allen, and Jonathan Baylis.

Thanks Mom and Dad and the rest of my wonderful family—not least my sister, Sara Castillo, who rocks it; doesn't stop it. Thanks to Todd Levin, for being a great friend, great advisor, and one of the greatest guys I know. To Ophira Eisenberg for being my partner in all endeavors creative and vodka related, for her singular and hilarious opinions, and for the title! Lastly, thanks to Jonathan Corbett, who gets top scores, and whose ear and ability to face my craziness with a Zenlike calm are invaluable to me.

AUTHOR'S NOTE

If you think any of the examples, stories, opinions, or . . . *incidents* in this book are based on you or someone you know, well, most of them aren't so flattering. You may want to work on that.

Contents

An Introduction

All's Fair
in Love and Score

I have the simplest tastes.
> I am always satisfied with the best.
> > —Oscar Wilde

You got an A-. . . . ? Why isn't it an A?
> —Fran and Ray Castillo

It often seems women are graded on a simple two-part scale: Salma Hayek, or not Salma Hayek. Meanwhile, like tourists traveling to heretofore uncharted corners of the globe, we buy dozens upon baker's dozens of books claiming they can safely guide us through the mysterious and dense land of How to Attract and Keep a Man. To survive in this land, you must be well-versed in its customs: Dress like Betty Crocker meets Bettie Page, laugh at his jokes, and don't expect him to ever call. So we run around— in heels, I might add—cutting, coloring, toning, tanning, pinching, painting, weighing, waxing, listening, and loving. In short: pleasing.

In the word of a Jennifer Lopez vehicle: *Enough*. Enough of fat older men with thin younger women every time you turn on the TV or watch a movie. Enough of your Jimmy Choos being treated like a pair of Skechers. (You walked around Saks every day for two weeks so you could get the best price on those shoes!) Enough of feeling if you just lost twenty pounds, none of the rest of it would matter.

So I pose a long-overdue question: Where is the book that helps us determine which men, if any, are worth our all-too-valuable time? (Did you hear me? *Two weeks* waiting on those shoes!) And I answer that question myself: right here, ladies, right here. It's time to turn the tables. And while we're at it, let's put a dozen doughnuts on those tables. 'Cause I love doughnuts.

Look at the type of advice so-called "relationship experts" are still giving women at this late date. *To reward him for using his fork, give him a sponge bath.* A sponge bath—am I a nurse in a VA hospital? *Wear clothes that accentuate his manly broad shoulders.* Ummm . . . a cheerleading uniform? *To get him to do housework, give him shiny things. He likes shiny things!* Am I dating someone developmentally disabled?

Don't get me wrong. I can imagine a scenario in which this advice would be helpful, like if I found it in a 1950's whorehouse. But last time I looked, men were still doing pretty well in our culture. Hold on, let me check. Yep, still kind of running things. Many of them seem incredibly capable and even (gasp!) intelligent. So why are we constantly being told we must treat them, and by extension, ourselves, like imbeciles? Why must we baby them while we tirelessly map out routes through our own impossible days—hold down full-time job, take dance class, start *hip* book club, regrout bathtub, finish master's thesis, rescue stray animals, decide whether to take teaching fellowship in Honduras—routes that at all costs must avoid passing establishments that sell cupcakes. After everything we do each day of every week, we still have to subscribe to a checklist of things that make him feel more manly?

Help is here. Like the phoenix rising up from the ashes (and like Phoenix rising up from the desert to become the sixth-largest city in America), so out of anger issues and an unhealthy attachment to vodka rises *The Score*. Each chapter of *The Score* will focus on a different aspect of the Guy, breaking it down in a systematic and thorough (capricious) fashion. Then, through a completely scientific and well-researched (random) system of quizzes and points, *The Score* will tell you without a doubt if the guy you're living with, dating, sleeping with, or erecting a secret shrine to is worth keeping around or chasing down. (Single ladies, get in here—it's never too soon to plan ahead!) And in case there's any doubt in your mind as to my expert credentials, I herein respectfully submit them for consideration. Many of my own relationships have been complete and utter disasters. Therefore, I promise to take no prisoners. Unless the guy is into that (see chapter six). So stop filling out coupons "good for one erotic massage" and putting "thanks for unclogging the sink" notes in his briefcase (backpack) and do something worthwhile with that pen. Put down your lip gloss and put up your feet. You've got some serious judging, I mean scoring, to do.

PART ONE

In the Beginning

Let's start from the very beginning, the place where there's still hope. Hope that when he gets up from the table he won't be wearing sandals with socks, hope that he doesn't talk about how much he misses *The Man Show* because it was the most brilliantly funny thing ever on television, hope that his idea of making conversation doesn't consist of staring at you until you say something. This is the first glow of the relationship when it's all exciting and new! When you think your cell phone might be vibrating, but it's just the beating of your heart!

When your friends can't stand to hear you say one more thing about him but they're too nice to tell you, so they just meet for drinks and complain about you! Fuck them. You're happy, and you listened to them talk about Neil and Kurt and . . . Baron. (Seriously, who's named Baron? Does he own a castle?)

But it's also the time to take stock quickly. To assess things before it's too late. To not be caught neck-high in water holding an umbrella, when you should have been running, screaming, "Flood!!" What if Ripley had had a book called *Grade the Possibility of Your Ship Being Infested by Aliens*? Would she have gotten on a ship with a robot? No. (Let me pause here and agree with you that not traveling with robots is just common sense, and a book might well be overkill.) Would she still have undressed into nothing but a T-shirt and an impossibly tiny pair of string bikini underpants (watch it again), oblivious to the alien lurking behind her in the machinery waiting to pounce? Even though she looked awesome, no. She would have taken the quiz and realized it was time to eject from that ship in the first five minutes of the film. But before you get all depressed that an alien is going to jump on your face and keep you in suspended animation until it finds another human host— *and isn't that just like an alien*—remember, the movie has a happy ending. She gets away, and she even keeps her cat. You might get to keep your guy.

Chapter 1

Judging the Look
by the Lover

style

In the words of ABC, "if you judge the book by the cover, then you'd judge the look by the lover." In our case, we'll start by judging the lover by his look. We all do it, and now let's all get over it. Before we know anything else about a guy, we know if we like what we see. It's later on, when we allow ourselves to be brainwashed by all the "women are less visually oriented than men" garbage, that we let these superficial criteria slide for other, seemingly more important things like emotional generosity and the ability to get through dinner with our parents. That's when we catch ourselves saying dangerous things like, "I kind of like his fleece zip-up vest. It's versatile!"

It's a simple fact—when it comes to fashion, men have it easier than we do. They can just throw on a pair of good jeans, a white T-shirt, and a decent pair of shoes and they look great. Hello, James Dean. This simple jeans/T-shirt/shoes calculation doesn't even require matching anything. So why are so many of them so challenged? Why do they go out in public wearing giant sports jerseys with someone else's name and number on them? How is it that the yellow shirt they always wear came out of a package marked "white"? Why do they expect their shoes should be comfortable? Why, when they have ten really nice shirts that you gave them right there in the closet do they always wear that one blue long-underwear shirt with the food stain on the front, dear God, why?

If you're one of those women who love fashion while resenting it slightly—you love to eat, and you don't make that much money—then you really appreciate it when a guy makes the effort to look good. It says that he understands that it's not just enough to *be* a man, even though signals he's given on a daily basis would lead him to believe differently. It says he wants to attract women and would like them to admire him. It's like he's reaching out across the great divide and saying, I kinda get what you're going through. It's a tip of the hat, if you will. With an actual hat. Let's look at a few possible styles one of these guys might sport.

Peter Fucking Pan

In springtime, a young lady's fancy turns to a tattoo sleeve. It's a throwback to the days when you used to date bass players. It was the age of foolishness, it was the age of foolishness. But the look plays on, and it goes a little something like this: A unique tattoo that he got before getting a tattoo became part of Hell Week at every fraternity in the country; straight-leg jeans that sit low but fit slim; Chuck Taylors, combat boots, or any member of the big black shoe family; a T-shirt that's somehow only ripped in appropriate places (not exposing an entire underarm or nipple); a jacket that looks like he might fix stuff for a living; and a good haircut. A Mohawk or a Fauxhawk or even a floppy "I'm so disappointed by the human race, I can only stand to look at the world with one eye so I cover the other with my hair" hawk. The kind of haircut that means he has a friend who works at a cool downtown salon. He obviously can't afford one. He's in a band.

F. Rap Fitzgerald

There is a hip-hop look that seems to have taken its cue from the music itself, sampling different styles. It's an Andre 3000, Common kind of hip-hop style. It's a Sean John, *Vanity Fair*, fashion of the Depression era dust bowl photo spread kind of style. There's usually a hat involved, perchance a fedora or *Newsies* cap, an argyle vest or maybe a buttoned-up shirt and tie, madras pants (*love* madras pants), a bright green jacket or a belted powder-blue one. If you're really lucky there may even be an entire plaid suit. And just when you think it can't get any better, are those saddle shoes? My God, they're saddle shoes. It's preppy, without all the messy "isms"—Protestantism, alcoholism, masochism. It takes a man of incredible confidence and vision to wear this look. Aka not white guys.

Check Them Out Now—The French Suit Brothers:

Just for argument's sake, let's say you end up with a guy who has a real job and has to wear a suit.

One summer, not so long ago, the French Suit Brothers were spotted frequently lunching in a park in New York City. They were probably not brothers, but they were definitely French. Even if you hadn't "accidentally" overheard their lilting accents, the way they wore their suits was a dead giveaway. What is it about French men and suits? They go together like junior high dances and awkward conversations. Each day they thrilled and awed with their bold choices of colors and patterns. Would they pair a striped shirt with a checked tie? Would green and greener rule the day? What's for lunch—azure and mustard? Tragically, before you could say, "Voulez-vous couchez avec moi, ce soir?" or even, "Oooh, la la!" the summer was gone and with it, the suits. Au revoir, les hommes. We'll always have Midtown.

Why is it when women have worked for years to develop what we delusionally consider to be our own personal style, we keep ending up with men who look like walking sidewalk sales? Who are these creatures who live among us, watching our TVs, reading our magazines, and looking at our billboards, yet seem strangely invulnerable to their influence? Is your guy one of the Style Immune? Or have you, by some lucky accident, found a guy who doesn't think shopping means he'll meet you at his favorite bar when you're done trying stuff on?

The Quiz: Wild Style

1. **When you look at your guy's hair, you think of:**

   a That guy I had a crush on in that band in college

   b U.S. Special Forces

   c The fact that my highlights need touching up and my ends are all frazzled

   d Robert Smith of The Cure

   e Michigan, the eighties, a tailgate party

2. **When you touch your guy's hair:**

   a It doesn't move. At all.

   b I can't stop

   c He freaks out and runs to the bathrooom to fix it

   d I get Manic Panic semipermanent dye all over my new shirt from H&M

   e I get a static electricity shock if I rub too long

3. **Around your guy's neck you'll find:**

   a An ascot

   b An Italian horn charm in fourteen-karat gold with a diamond chip in the center

   c My arms

d Puka shells

e An albatross

4. Your guy dresses to show off his:

    a Ability to match anything with brown

    b Eighteenth-century sensibility

    c Ass—his pants are always tighter than mine . . .

    d "Kill 'em all, let God sort 'em out" tattoo

    e Personality

5. Which song best represents your guy's style:

    a "Harley David Son of a Bitch" by Serge Gainsbourg

    b "Sharp Dressed Man" by ZZ Top

    c "Love Will Tear Us Apart" by Joy Division

    d "Hip to Be Square" by Huey Lewis and the News

    e Any song by Bob Seger and the Silver Bullet Band

6. Your guy getting dressed up for a night out means:

    a He gets to wear the new pants that we bought together and that shirt he knows I like

    b "I hope I have something clean. Oh, here's something under the coffee table!"

    c A phone call to his personal shopper

d Black . . . like his heart, like his soul, like his life

e Calling his best friend to make sure he's not wearing that shiny shirt that zips up the front they both bought at Fantasions in the mall

7. The one thing that your guy wears that you never want to see again is:

a The T-shirt with the picture of his dog on it

b The T-shirt with my baby picture on it

c The Alien Sex Fiend Club T-shirt

d The Ten Reasons a Beer Is Better than a Woman T-shirt

e The limited edition "This Is Not a T-shirt" T-shirt

8. When the invitation says "jacket required," your guy shows up in:

a Members Only

b A paisley tuxedo

c His favorite jean jacket from high school

d A nice jacket that belonged to his father

e A frock coat

9. By the sea, by the sea, this is what you see:

a A pair of eyes peering out from beneath the hat and umbrella

b Colorful swim trunks that hit at the knee

c A male bikini

d Five-year-old board shorts that are a *liiiitle* too tight

e Jean cutoffs and a six-pack of Michelob

10. Most "eye-catching" pair of shoes in your guy's closet are:

a Handmade sandals from Brazil, where he spent several years as a child because his father works for the government

b Do Tevas count as shoes . . . ?

c Spiderweb combat boots

d Vintage Jon Fluevogs he can't part with

e Biker boots—with real spurs!

Sure, you think you see exactly where we're going with this quiz, but don't get too comfortable, because it's only going to get harder from here. And don't cheat. Cheating hurts all of us. Particularly you.

The Score

1. a 5, b 4, c 3, d 2, e 1
2. a 1, b 5, c 3, d 2, e 4
3. a 3, b 1, c 5, d 4, e 2

4.	a 4,	b 2,	c 3,	d 1,	e 5
5.	a 3,	b 5,	c 2,	d 4,	e 1
6.	a 5,	b 4,	c 3,	d 2,	e 1
7.	a 4,	b 5,	c 2,	d 1,	e 3
8.	a 1,	b 3,	c 4,	d 5,	e 2
9.	a 2,	b 5,	c 3,	d 4,	e 1
10.	a 3,	b 4,	c 2,	d 5,	e 1

43–50: Looking good, feeling good!

Your guy gets it. He may have looked at a magazine or two, or noticed what a favorite actor or band was wearing. Maybe he just took the time to notice when you gave him a compliment. He's stylish without being a slave to fashion, and what he wears reflects who he is. Just as important, you like how he looks. It makes you want to give him a big, fat hug.

34–42: There's a light.

Dear *The Score* Forum, I never thought I'd be the kind of girl to write a letter like this, but you can change the way he dresses. It's not a full-on attack, it's just a tweak here and there. If he has a decent haircut and one or two decent shirts, you can make subtle suggestions or just buy him good gifts for his birthday or the holidays or Thursday. Don't push too hard, just see what he's comfortable with. Take heart. Other women have done it successfully and guys have gone from completely fashion challenged to walking down the street proudly chanting, "I got a new shirt!" Hey, it's a start.

26–33: Down a notch.

OK, seriously, unless he's a model or a professional ballroom dancer, your guy needs to butch it up a bit. Actually, especially if he's a professional ballroom dancer. A guy can be a little too femme, and this guy is. He should be able to deal with the occasional hair tussle, and what's with the tight pants?

*Question exception: For Down a Notch if your guy is European, you're allowed to add 5 points to his score, but only because he really doesn't know any better.

18–25: The dead come home.

It's a rule as old and pointless as human suffering itself: once a Goth, always a Goth. I don't know . . . maybe hide his pancake makeup?

10–17: Married to the mob.

Move to New Jersey. Go with God. Or with really big, dark sunglasses.

Chapter 1 score: _____

Cumulative score: _____
(Hint: for this chapter they're the same.)

Birkenstocks. What was that you said? Oh, they're hip now? You saw a picture in a magazine and John Cusack was wearing them? No, really, OK, I get it, I guess they're cool!

I'm glad you're not a lamb. Because if you were a lamb, right about now you'd be thinking, why am I standing in this line and why is every lamb at the front of the line screaming? I don't want to hear it because I've already seen it. I've seen the fancy Birkenstocks, fashioned by elves out of pure gold and sold at a 5,000 percent markup to ensure that the hippies who invented them in the first place could never afford them. And guess what? They're still ugly. They are quite simply the ugliest shoe known to man. And when I say man, I mean Man. Men are not allowed to wear sandals ever. You know who wore sandals all the time? Jesus. And look what happened to him. Walk away from the Mandals. You won't even have to walk that fast, because the guy will be slowed down by stepping daintily around puddles and making sure gravel doesn't get stuck between his toes. How arrogant does a guy have to be to say, "Hey, I'm so hot, I can ignore millions of years of fashion oppression and wear a formless anti-clog held to my naked foot by two straps of buckled suede"? No one is that hot.

He's Wearing	You're Hearing
Black turtleneck tucked into black satin pleated pants, a white belt, tan Capezios	I just came from auditions for a Fosse musical, and now I can go straight to my job waiting tables without changing!
A giant sports jersey, giant jeans, giant sneakers, Number-One foam finger	I have constructed a fantasy life in my head in which I'm not winded when I walk up a flight of stairs.
A giant sports jersey, giant jeans, giant sneakers, gem-encrusted medallion of Jesus	Foshizzle ma nizzle?
A dark purple shirt, a yellow tie, bright orange pants	I'm color-blind, and my friends are assholes.
Leather pants and cowboy boots	Which way to the '80s, padner?
Year-round tan	Nothing can harm me. I am immortal!
Fake tan	No one will date me. I am lonely!
Biking shorts	Nothing embarrasses me. I am sexy.
Levis, ironic T-shirt, red, white, and blue striped sweat wristband, ironic trucker cap, aviator sunglasses (worn with total irony, 'cause it's raining)	I live in Williamsburg. The cool one. In Brooklyn.
Paper jeans, Penguin shirt, Ben Sherman jacket, New Balance sneakers, Von Dutch hat	I live in Williamsburg off my trust fund.

He's Wearing	You're Hearing
Ermenegildo Zegna suit, Armani shirt and tie, Bruno Magli shoes, Patek Philippe watch	I make shitloads of money and very little conversation.
Loafers with no socks	Hey, I can get as Casual Friday as the next guy, my man.
Cat in the Hat hat, glow sticks, pacifier	I'm sooo dehydrated. . . . What day is it?
Long hair, goatee or soul patch or extreme sideburns, wool hat with medieval cross in summer, wallet with chain, biker boots	Satan is my master . . . right after I finish delivering these packages.
Top hat, cane, long black cape	The Phannnntom of the Oper-a is here in Starbucks!
Camouflage pants, camouflage jacket, camouflage hat, army surplus combat boots	Private Minimum Wage, reporting for service, sir!
Linen suit, white bucks, straw hat	I'm "Southern," like Truman Capote . . .
Zoo York T-shirt, straight-leg ladies' jeans, Ipath sneakers, gray hoodie, Yankees cap	Dude, this totally reminds me of that scene in *Dogtown and Z-Boys*!

CHAPTER 2

THE SEARCH FOR SIGNS OF INTELLIGENT LIFE

 His Mind

If there's one pair of pants all the women I know are looking for, it's the smarty-pants. In fact, many women I know feel like they need to be with a man who's smarter than they are. This may come from the glorious notion that's programmed into us that the guy should do the thinkin' and we should sit there and be purty. Or the insecurity that not being as smart as us might mean not being smart at all. Or in some cases, sheer laziness.

Having said that, beware the Know-It-All. By definition, the Know-It-All has to be certain *you* know he knows it all. Where will the torture end? With you looking around the room, making signals to your friends that you think mean "Get over here right now and save me from Professor Prat," but they think mean "This could be The One!" (You might want to agree on those signals before you go out next time.) The Know-It-All runs the gamut, from the guy who instructs you while dancing at a club, "I'm not Mod. I'm French New Wave," to the guy who informs you on a first date your vocabulary is weak and you should not use the same adjective more than once in a night's conversation. A good friend used to date a guy who would try to prove you wrong just for the sake of being right. No matter what you did, he would push the argument, even if you were attempting to gracefully let it go. What follows is a transcript of a True-Life Argument with this man.

> ME: "Hey, I heard a cool cover of Funkadelic's 'Free Your Mind and Your Ass Will Follow.'"
>
> HIM: "No. It's called 'Free Your Ass and Your Mind Will Follow.'"
>
> ME: "Really, are you sure? 'Cause I think it's 'Free Your Mind' . . ." (drifting off, trying to let it go).
>
> HIM: "Bet you a dollar."
>
> ME: "It really doesn't matter."
>
> HIM: "Bet you two!"

(Just for the record, I was right. I'm totally over it, though.)

Hey, Conan the Librarian, calm down. Knowledge should not be used as a weapon with which to smite all who go against you so you can hear the lamentations of their women. Of course you want a guy who has knowledge to spare and knowledge to share, who can engage in lively debates about music, movies, film, literature, and what's left of music video with you. But there's a difference between an equal exchange of ideas and feeling like you have to hit him on the hand and yell "tag out!" every time you want to make a point. It's so basic, ladies—a guy who's secure with his intelligence won't have to spend precious make-out time lecturing you on the mechanics of a rare organ used on certain blues recordings from the years 1954 to 1962.

And then there are those of you who, after a night of talking about what your beer tastes like in painstaking detail, find yourself repeating this mantra: "But he's really nice." "He has hair." "He exists!" Yes, he very well may possess one or all of those qualities, right down to the full head of hair, but is that enough for you? Does he have some other talent that might make up for his lacking brilliance? Maybe he can build a cabin or lift a lot of weight all at once or drive the cattle into town to sell them. And if you're in a production of *Oklahoma!*, obsessed with the film *Pumping Iron*, or in yet another production of *Oklahoma!,* those abilities might come in really handy. But what happens when bodybuilders trade in their gym memberships for political offices or when the bright golden haze on the meadow turns to darkness? Do you really want to spend weeks, months, possibly years, saying, "So . . . Britney Spears got another divorce!" in an attempt to find something to talk about?

Even if your guy has just won the Nobel Peace prize, I'd

be willing to bet that gold medal that he's still flummoxed when it comes to things that matter to you. Even Stephen Hawking is infamous for his troubles with the ladies. Sure, we could test him on where all the different countries go on a map and in how many languages he can say "I'm not sure I'm ready to commit." Sure, we could make him quote lines from Shakespeare or *Heat*. But any guy with a reasonable amount of brains could come through with that. How many of them can answer the kind of questions most women can answer in their sleep? Put yourself in your guy's shoes. Literally, if that's what it takes. Become your guy. Sit in front of the TV and flip through all the channels three times in a row at lightning speed. Sit at the dinner table and spread your legs to take up two spaces. Sit in the balcony at the ballet and fall asleep. Then, answer the following questions as he would.

The Quiz: Do You Know What I Know?

1. **Where is Saks Fifth Avenue located?**

   a Fifth Avenue. By the way, that's hilarious.

   b In which city?

   c In Macy's

2. **The ingredients in a Cosmopolitan are:**

   a Vodka, triple sec, dash of cranberry juice, fresh lime juice

   b Alcohol, sweet tarts, and $12

   c A bunch of quizzes about how to please me in bed

3. French tips are:

a Paid in francs

b A white line over the ends of your nails in a manicure

c "Zare is no need to takay ze bath ev-ay-ry day"

4. Susan B. Anthony appears on the:

a WB

b Cover of *W* this month

c Dollar coin

5. Finish this poem: Faith is a fine invention for gentlemen who see.

But microscopes are prudent in _____.

a A crystal meth lab

b An emergency

c An episode of *Law & Order: SVU*

6. *Sense and Sensibility* is:

a A good thing to have when you're buying pot

b A great movie starring Hugh Grant

c A novel by Jane Austen

7. **Christian Louboutin, Edmundo Castillo, and Miu Miu make:**

   a Fabulous shoes

   b Not sure, but it sounds like a drag act

   c My parent's summer home on Block Island clean?

8. **The Curse of the Bambino was:**

   a My uncle's homemade hot sauce

   b The reason the Red Sox sucked for more than eighty years

   c A western starring Jane Russell

9. **Sporty, Scary, Baby, Posh, and Ginger are:**

   a On that poster in your bedroom

   b The Spice Girls!

   c Things you can put in your soy sauce at a Japanese restaurant

10. **Name the fearless single-horned animal that only a pure maiden can ensnare:**

    a Unicorn

    b Sixteen-year-old guy

    c Kenny G

I I. What is brunch?

  a A pain in the ass

  b The meal that combines breakfast and lunch and takes three hours to eat

  c The most important meal on *Sex and the City*

I 2. Book that is first in a series about a rebellious redheaded orphan adopted by a spinster and her brother on Prince Edward Island:

  a *Molly Ringwald: A Biography*

  b *Anne of Green Gables*

  c *Lucille Ball: A Biography*

I 3. Finish this book title: *Are You There God? It's Me,*

  a Pete Rose

  b Jesus

  c Margaret

I 4. What is Bonne Bell known for?

  a Lip Smackers in delicious flavors like bubble gum and Tootsie Roll

  b Sewing the first American flag

  c Being the first Miss Italy to win Miss Universe

15. What does a blowout usually cost you?

a The keys to my parents' summer home on Block Island

b Anywhere from twenty to one hundred dollars, depending on the salon

c I told you, I've never paid for sex!

The Score

1.	a 2,	b 3,	c 1
2.	a 3,	b 2,	c 1
3.	a 2,	b 3,	c 1
4.	a 1,	b 3,	c 2
5.	a 3,	b 2,	c 1
6.	a 1,	b 3,	c 2
7.	a 3,	b 2,	c 1
8.	a 1,	b 3,	c 2
9.	a 2,	b 3,	c 1
10.	a 3,	b 2,	c 1
11.	a 1,	b 2,	c 3
12.	a 2,	b 3,	c 1
13.	a 1,	b 2,	c 3
14.	a 3,	b 2,	c 1
15.	a 1,	b 3,	c 2

36–45: Which team?

Either he has a ton of sisters or he is a sister. Boy, this guy sure knows a lot about the feminine side of life. I have to say it, lady . . . You may be dating a gay man. So even though he gets big points for knowing shoe designers and unicorns, his answer to *Sense and Sensibility* might make you think twice. (Coincidentally, *Shoe Designers and Unicorns* is the title of my memoir.) And hey, if you are dating a gay man, no one's judging you. It's a time-tested tradition. After all, at least nine women I know can't be wrong!

25–35: Social promotion.

He knows Susan B. Anthony is on the dollar coin, so he probably went to high school. He knows the ending to an Emily Dickinson poem. So he probably went to college. When it comes to general knowledge, this guy is doing all right. But maybe he could know a little bit more about where you're coming from. Some of his answers are right-on. Some even demonstrate a grudging willingness to occasionally pay attention. He just needs some adult education in all things Lady.

15–24: Arm candy!

That's right, my lady. I don't know how you get any quality time with him while constantly running away from the paparazzi. Because your guy is a looker! He's a freaking male model. At least he better be, with these answers. Go to Greece with him. Dance barefoot under the stars. Roll around in the sand with him. Dump him when you get back.

Chapter 2 score: _____

Cumulative score: _____

Getting the Last Word In

Smarts. Sometimes the word means something hurts. Too much knowledge can potentially be an annoying thing. Have you ever been with that guy who makes you feel like shit by incredulously exclaiming, "You've never read Bukowski?" as if you just told him you never learned to use a toilet so instead you wear a diaper like a monkey? Then there's the conspiracy theorist who doesn't believe in the moon landing but who does believe in aliens. He knows everything about a lot of things that probably didn't even happen, but he can't seem to keep your friends from mysteriously disappearing whenever you're all out together. Or how about that guy with weird niche knowledge—the history of every state capital memorized in alphabetical order!—who not only imagines other people are interested in what he knows, but just loves to lecture anyone who will listen! Ever tried to joke around with a language poet? Can't be done. I'll prove it. "Hey, Language Poet: Why did the chicken cross the road?" Answer: "Chair chair credenza of the moon Robitussin rounds the bend of mending hearts, parts part." See what I mean? Imagine what happens when you ask one if he can pass the salt.

Knowledge is something not only of quantity but of quality. Not only of a degree but of degree. A self-educated guy can be just as intellectually curious, knowledgeable, and interesting to talk to as a college-educated guy. If everyone who went to college were so freaking smart, where would legacy kids go? Intelligence is like a jukebox—we may all start with four quarters, but what we end up with is vastly different. One person puts in her quarters and plays "Rock You Like a Hurricane," another plays "Wind Beneath My Wings." But no matter what you want out of it, you need to find someone who can rock with you and also picks new songs that enrich your listening experience. Hmm . . . A15 . . . what's that? "Sweet Child O' Mine"? Awesome.

The Score Study Guide for Guys:
Essential Knowledge He Needs to Know You

Study Tool	Lesson
The Bell Jar	Sometimes a girl gets down. Real down.
The Smiths	Don't go home tonight. Go out and find the one that you love and who loves you!
Destiny's Child	I don't think you're ready for this jelly.
Madonna	If we took a holiday (oh yeah, oh yeah), just some time to celebrate (come on, let's celebrate), just *one* day out of life (Ho-li-day), it would be—it would be—so nice.

Study Tool	Lesson
Ice Castles	When you go blind, you still have to skate Nationals.
Dirty Dancing	Nobody puts Baby in a corner.
The Way We Were	Can it be that it was all so simple then? Um. No.
Bring It On	Don't ever let the spirit stick touch the ground!
Grease	In the '50s people went to high school in their thirties.
Fame	The cafeteria's not a place to eat. It's a place to *dance*.
Katharine Hepburn	It's great to wear the pants in the family.
Audrey Hepburn	True glamour does not require implants.
Wonder Woman	If there's one thing that goes perfectly with bullet-deflecting bracelets, it's a gold lasso.
Love Story	Love means never having to say you're sorry.
Judy Blume	It's not *really* forever.
Mae West	An ounce of performance is worth pounds of promises.

CHAPTER 3

WHAT'S SO FUNNY?

 sense of Humor

How many times have you heard it? "You really made me laugh. I don't usually find women funny." Cue the choir of angels: *Aaaah-aaaaah!* And now, knowing you have made a man laugh, you can die. There's a myth that men are funnier than women. That's what it is. A myth. Just as much a myth as the one about the guy who looked at his reflection in the water so long that he fell in love with himself. OK, maybe not the best example because I can kind of see that happening.

Truth be told, we don't really find men as funny as we'd have them believe, do we? Raise your hand if you've ever laughed at a guy when you didn't think he was funny. (I had to stop typing for a minute.) Think about the serious consequences of that action. But sometimes laughing at something you don't find funny is like eating something you hate at a dinner party. Even though it makes you sick to your stomach, it's just easier to do.

All of my close friendships and long-term relationships have been with guys with great senses of humor, as well as many one-night stands. (Call me, Carrot Top!) But even the most intelligent men seem to find the same childish things funny. Somewhere at NASA right now, a physicist is making a fart noise with his hands in time to an astronaut walking down the hall, and the rocket scientist with him is cracking up, tears streaming down his face. Even a guy whose jokes are smart will still laugh hysterically when he sees a dog wearing sunglasses, thereby forcing you to put on sunglasses of your own to shield yourself from this horrible truth.

What follows are examples of witticism that every time a guy executes, the woman who witnesses them gets a look in her eyes somewhere between "I swear I don't know how these drugs got in my bags. Please let me call my lawyer," and "Can I change my hair drastically enough that no one here would ever recognize me again?"

The Screamer:
It's hilarious when I yell something over and over that only my friends understand at a party or in a crowded bar. It's even better if I can get all my friends to yell it, too. It's like a cult, but funny.

Gregarious Guy:
Hey, I don't know you, but I'm going to involve you in my conversation because it's even funnier if I interrupt your conversation and pretend we're all in on the joke, right? Oh, and also because I'm an egomaniac.

Waitresses Think I'm Hilarious:
Newsflash: They don't.

Pretending to Be Gay Guy:
Pretending I'm going to kiss my friends is funny 'cause I'm straight that's why I pretend like I'm going to have gay sex with my friends all the time because it's hilarious and I'm straight so if I pretend to grab my straight guy friend's ass or act like I'm stroking his nipple it's super funny 'cause I'm really straight. Straight.

Hidden Anger Guy:
That dress makes you look fat. Just kidding. But seriously, does Ringling Brothers still have a tent?

The Merry Prankster:
Dude, did you see Kevin try to pick up that girl with his fly open? It was awesome! Aaaaand high five.

Lowest common denominator isn't the only challenge. What about reciprocation? Does he laugh at your jokes? It's hard to be with a guy who smiles politely or even cringes slightly when you try to join in on the joke, and then goes back to trading punch lines with his friends. Or what about the guy who gives lip service to the idea that women are funny but secretly thinks, "but not as funny as guys." How about the guys who think it's hilarious to put each other down, but the moment you join in grow suddenly sensitive? And then there's the guy who thinks it's OK for you to be funny, as long as you don't get bigger laughs than he does. Or the crown jewel, the guy who is under the weird misapprehension that all women joke about is their periods. As if guys don't make dick jokes, by the way. A guy who can't or won't appreciate your sense of humor is like the inside of a litter box in a household of slobs: shitty.

Still, most women claim to prize a sense of humor in a guy above all else. So much so that you see fantastic women hang on every word of men who wouldn't get a second look without it. If you're one of those women who's willing to put humor first and sacrifice all else for it, think about listening to your guy's bits, day after day, night after night, after-party after after-party. Is there some common ground? Is he funny enough for *you*, or does he just joke about the same stuff guys always joke about—robots, pirates, his balls.

The Quiz: Oh My God, That's So Funny!

Here's a random sampling of things people might find funny. Check any and all that regularly make your guy laugh.

___ *The Office* (British)

___ Wedgies (regular and atomic)

___ Molly Shannon

___ *Insomniac*

___ *Mr. Show*

___ *The Carol Burnett Show*

___ Prank phone calls

___ Amy Sedaris

___ *Jackass*

___ *Blue Collar TV*

___ *Absolutely Fabulous*

___ *Will & Grace*

___ Your cat

___ The word *taint*

___ The oeuvre of Kevin Smith

___ Monkeys dressed as humans

___ Burping/farting in public

___ Stupid puns

___ *Sex and the City*

___ Woody Allen films up to and including *Crimes and Misdemeanors*

___ *Arrested Development*

___ *This Is Spinal Tap*

___ Tina Fey

___ Fake punching

___ Ellen DeGeneres

___ Midget wrestling

___ *The Howard Stern Show*

___ *The Daily Show*

___ *The Man Show*

___ Will Ferrell movies

The Score

Boy Humor 0

___ Jackass

___ The Howard Stern Show

___ The word *taint*

___ The oeuvre of Kevin Smith

___ Burping/farting in public

___ Prank phone calls

___ The Man Show

___ Blue Collar TV

___ Wedgies (regular and atomic)

___ Midget wrestling

Common Ground + 5

___ Insomniac

___ Monkeys dressed as humans

___ The Office (British)

___ Fake punching

___ Arrested Development

___ Mr. Show

___ This Is Spinal Tap

___ The Daily Show

___ Woody Allen films up to and including *Crimes and Misdemeanors*

___ Will Ferrell movies

Bonus Lady Laughs + 10

___ The Carol Burnett Show

___ Absolutely Fabulous

___ Will & Grace

___ Your cat

___ Ellen DeGeneres

___ Amy Sedaris

___ Sex and the City

___ Molly Shannon

___ Stupid puns

___ Tina Fey

75–150: Two ladies walk into a bar.

Wow, your guy has very sophisticated taste. He enjoys humor that only we ladies are generally evolved enough to appreciate. Come on, your cat is hilarious! Take a bow, sir, nicely played. However, monkeys are really, really funny. Have you ever seen one dressed as a doctor? Or a ballerina? Just checking.

25–70: He looks kind of funny.

And I mean that in the nicest of ways. This guy is a good balance of things that you both find funny in common and the occasional embarrassing public display with his friends. But the point is, he doesn't shut you out. You can laugh with each other. You probably think fake punching is kind of funny now, don't you?

0–20: You can't be serious.

Really? You share a sense of humor with this guy? There may be nothing I can do to save you, nothing I can say to help you. They say humor is subjective, and I subjectively find his sense of humor to be seriously juvenile. But if you're into totally cracking up over "What is up with women leaving their tampons where we can see them?" and "Here's Arnold Schwarzenegger giving head" for the rest of your life, well, then, I'm truly sorry for you.

Chapter 3 score: _____

Cumulative score: _____

Getting the Last Word In

Gallagher & Gallagher II are both guys. Draw your own conclusions.

CHAPTER 4

WHEN A STRANGER CALLS

 Dating

First, we all need to agree on what constitutes a date. You're a modern lady. No one rides up to your door in a carriage with a calling card, requesting the honor of your company for a weekend party at a country estate. More likely, the "honor of your company" refers to an incident at your office holiday party with someone from Finance. In the ever-changing landscape of male-female relationships, sometimes it's hard to remember what "dating" even means. The concept seems almost antiquated and formal. It brings to mind a gentler time, before cell phones, when you actually had to make (and keep) plans. The idea that you might risk wasting actual time getting to know someone outside of a chat room is astounding. But people are still doing it, so let's agree *none* of the following qualifies as a date:

Being asked to join his Friendster list

Meeting in line for the bathroom at a party

Tutoring him in English as a second language

A sorority party (even if the theme is Island Romance)

Doing your laundry in the basement at the same time he does

Getting an autographed picture after his show

Singing along to "American Pie" with his folk guitar around a campfire

Stripping at his bachelor party

Hanging out with him and his friends all night, then having drunken sex

Hanging out with him and his friends at Bible study, then sharing pie in the rectory (no, that is not a metaphor for sex!)

Like many crimes, a date requires premeditation. It's you and him, sharing quality time together, getting to know one another (or not, as the case may be). You may be seeing a movie or eating a fancy dinner or meeting for a drink at a dive bar or playing a game of pool, but it's you and him—not you, him, and his poker buddies. Yes, sometimes there may be TV cameras and physical challenges involved, but we'll overlook that for the sake of the cash prize. Yes, it can be nerve-wracking and scary, but no matter how unpredictable the outcome, dating can also be exciting. From flirting to being asked out to putting your get-ready music on the stereo and trying on seven different outfits to the first good-night kiss, there's nothing quite like the anticipation of the event. It's like your own personal *Star Wars* premiere. And just like *Star Wars* premieres, you'll probably end up having more of them than you'd ever think necessary. So although you sometimes hate it and you find it frustrating, relish it while you can. Chances are you'll miss it when it's gone.

Hey, ladies in relationships—don't think you're getting left out on this one. I bet you met your current boyfriend by going on a few dates with him. A committed relationship shouldn't mean committed to the exile of your apartment and take-out menus. Every once in a while, you should revive the dating ritual by going lip to lip and breathing new life into it. Go on a date! Get dressed up, make a reservation that doesn't have to do with whether he's right for you, meet somewhere you've never been before, and resuscitate all those feelings you had when you first met. You might even have wild sex again. Or at least have sex again.

The Quiz: It's a Date!

1. To meet you, he:

a Asks friends for an introduction

b Walks up to me and strikes up conversation

c Stays super-late at the bar to sees who's left and who's drunk

d Throws a napkin at my head from across the bar and yells, "Two points!"

2. He flirts by:

a Asking, "Hey, do you name your breasts?"

b Sending me a drink

c Sexy-dancing around me, while "I Want It That Way" plays on the jukebox

d Making me laugh

3. His online profile says he's looking for:

a A smart, challenging woman who shares common interests and goals

b Someone who's not always bugging him when the game is on

c Someone who makes him laugh and doesn't remind him of his mother

d Jenna Jameson

4. To ask you out, he:

   a Sends me a flyer to come see his band

   b Asks for my number and calls me

   c E-mails me a few times, then writes, "We should meet"

   d Rolls over and says, "What's your name again?"

5. You ask him if he's involved with anyone. His response:

   a "What my wife doesn't know won't hurt her!"

   b He ceases to make eye contact and starts to stutter

   c "No"

   d "Hopefully you"

6. You're setting the date! He:

   a Suggests a place he likes, taking into account my preferences

   b Asks for my address and what kind of pizza I like

   c Chooses a place to meet

   d Says, "Cool. Um, so what should we do?"

7. The celebrity he most reminds you of:

   a Denzel Washington

   b Luke Wilson

c Colin Farrell

d Crispin Glover

8. You meet for drinks and he:

a Orders a drink, and lets me order mine

b Is already drunk off his ass when I arrive

c Lines up shots of tequila along the bar and says, "Race ya!"

d Orders for me, allowing me to find a place to sit

9. Another man interrupts your conversation with a flirty comment. He:

a Says, "Wow. We were just talking about how much we don't like people who interrupt"

b Jokes around with the guy and buys him drinks—all night

c Listens politely, then steers me to another spot

d Starts a bar fight, chair first

10. Unexpectedly, friends of his are at the bar. He:

a Strikes up a game of foosball with them, leaving me sitting at the bar

b Grabs my hand and pulls me out of the bar, saying, "I don't want to see those assholes" c Introduces them, then excuses the two of us

    d Strikes up conversation, starting with "This is the woman I was telling you about"

11. You have too many Jäger shots and pass out, head on the table. He:

    a Makes absolutely sure I get home safely

    b Hits the dance floor—there are some hotties out there

    c Puts me in a cab, giving the driver twenty dollars and my address

    d Pins a note to me that reads, "Wake me when it's over"

12. You meet him for dinner and are surprised to see him:

    a Waiting for me because he arrived early

    b Flirting with the sexy bartender

    c Asking for a better table

    d Hugging his mom

13. When you receive your menus he:

    a Keeps commenting on how expensive everything is

    b Talks knowledgeably about the choices and makes suggestions c Says, "Just so long as you don't order beans!" (fart noise)

   d Pays more attention to me than the menu

14. When the food arrives he:

   a Makes sure I have everything I need and our drinks are refreshed

   b Reaches across the table and grabs a forkful

   c Waits until everything arrives and I start eating before he does

   d Says, "Wow . . . are you going to eat *all* that?"

15. You're not crazy about your food. He:

   a Says, "Really? Huh. I like this place"

   b Says, "That's OK. I'll take it to go"

   c Immediately flags the waiter and asks for something different

   d Apologizes and asks if I'd like to order something else

16. Describe his eating style:

   a Emily Post would be jealous

   b My mom would be satisfied

   c "Slap some more vittles on my plate, Cookie, I'm starvin'"

   d Hot-dog eating competition champion

1 7. When you're talking to him you feel like:

   a He's performing for an audience of one

   b He's really trying to get to know me and wants to tell me about himself

   c I'm conducting an interview about his "fascinating" life for a news program called "No One Cares"

   d No one else is in the room

1 8. Someone calls him on his cell during dinner. He:

   a Answers it, mouths, "I'll be right back," and walks outside to have the conversation

   b Turns it off apologetically, ignoring the call

   c Doesn't know because he turned it off and put it away

   d Answers it and says, "Nah, nothing important. I'll be outta here soon"

1 9. During the meal, you excuse yourself to go to the bathroom. He:

   a Jokes, "Hey, I'll meet you in there in five minutes." (Wink)

   b Stands up from the table when I leave and return

   c Tells me to hurry back

   d Yells, "Let me know how it comes out!" after me

20. He treats the staff at the restaurant:

a In a friendly manner, making conversation and joking

b Like they're members of a loud, unruly family at Thanksgiving dinner: "Hey! Can I get a fork here?"

c With respect, always saying please and thank you

d Like he's royalty and this is his "help"

21. The check comes:

a After some convincing, he lets me leave the tip

b He counts out his half and throws it on the table

c He picks it up and pays, despite any offer to split it

d He takes out a calculator and says, "We're splitting the appetizer, right?"

22. In the wee hours of the morning, you somehow find yourself singing karaoke. He:

a Manages to get the whole bar singing "New York, New York"

b Doesn't sing

c Sings a duet with me, despite his inability to carry a tune

d Performs a song dedicated to me, substituting blue lyrics for the real ones

23. The date is winding down, the vibe is good. He:

    a Lunges down my throat via his tongue

    b Offers me a mint

    c Leans in and kisses me, then says good night

    d Says, "I'd really like to kiss you"

24. The date is over. He:

    a Makes sure I'm safely in a cab, car, at my train

    b High-fives me and leaves me at the curb

    c Turns around and walks back into the bar

    d Offers to walk me home, even after he finds out I live in Brooklyn

25. He says he'll call you:

    a He calls a couple of days later

    b He doesn't, but I run into him and he asks to see me again

    c He calls me a month later to tell me about his art opening

    d He calls the next day

The Score

1. **a** 3, **b** 4, **c** 2, **d** 1
2. **a** 1, **b** 4, **c** 2, **d** 3
3. **a** 4, **b** 2, **c** 3, **d** 1
4. **a** 2, **b** 4, **c** 3, **d** 1
5. **a** 1, **b** 2, **c** 4, **d** 3
6. **a** 3, **b** 1, **c** 4, **d** 2
7. **a** 4, **b** 3, **c** 2, **d** 1
8. **a** 3, **b** 1, **c** 2, **d** 4
9. **a** 3, **b** 2, **c** 4, **d** 1
10. **a** 1, **b** 2, **c** 4, **d** 3
11. **a** 4, **b** 2, **c** 3, **d** 1
12. **a** 3, **b** 2, **c** 4, **d** 1
13. **a** 2, **b** 4, **c** 1, **d** 3
14. **a** 4, **b** 2, **c** 3, **d** 1
15. **a** 2, **b** 1, **c** 4, **d** 3
16. **a** 4, **b** 3, **c** 2, **d** 1
17. **a** 2, **b** 3, **c** 1, **d** 4
18. **a** 2, **b** 3, **c** 4, **d** 1
19. **a** 2, **b** 4, **c** 3, **d** 1
20. **a** 3, **b** 2, **c** 4, **d** 1

21.	a	3,	b	2,	c	4,	d	1
22.	a	2,	b	4,	c	3,	d	1
23.	a	2,	b	1,	c	4,	d	3
24.	a	4,	b	2,	c	1,	d	3
25.	a	3,	b	0,	c	0,	d	4

82–100: Does he have a brother?

This is pretty much the dream date. This guy is good. He's super-attentive and polite. He cares about treating you well and making sure you have a good time. Here's the only catch: He may be too formal, a little too old school, a tad too solicitous. After all, you can flag down the waiter, too, and split the check if that's your preference. Loosen up a little. Everyone likes karaoke, right? Still, great big points for being a total gentleman and covering all the bases.

62–81: One more time.

This guy is great! He may not dot every i and cross every room to open the door for you, but he's trying. He's fun to be around. He diffuses tense situations by using his sense of humor and social skills. When he messes up, he finds a way to make it OK. I like him. You like him. See him again.

43–61: Clueless, dude.

If you want to be someone's mom, without all that messy giving birth stuff date this guy. Sometimes instead of buying a drink for everyone in the bar, he could check in on you. Yes, he can be fun to hang out with, his little-boy-lost quality can be endearing, and he can make it seem like he'll change. But the minute you walk out the door, he's practicing the bass again.

24–42: *Cauchemar!* (Nightmare!)

Never speak to the person who set you up with this guy again. If you are even thinking of going out with him again, minus a kabillion points and shame, shame, shame—shame on you.

---

*Question exception: If you answered (b) or (c) to question 25 about calling you and you are still seeing this guy, subtract 500 points. Yep, that's that. No, you can't dig him out of that hole, nor should you be able to.

Chapter 4 score: _____

Cumulative score: _____

Getting the Last Word In

You're out with friends, the check arrives, and your guy immediately starts listing how much each person at the table ate and what each person owes. You're going to a friend's house for dinner, and he picks out the week-old flowers because even though they look a little brown around the edges, they're marked down. Everyone's buying a round of drinks, except your guy, who manages to get quietly drunk all the same. You're taking a trip, and you have to go on the six A.M. flight to save thirty dollars, then wait hours to check into your hotel.

A little bird told me something, lady. What's that he's saying? Your guy is "Cheap . . . cheapcheapcheap! Cheap!"

There is nothing worse than a cheap guy. It's like nails on a blackboard. And he's not going to spend the money to fix your manicure. A cheap guy is going to cost you extra hassle and ultimately embarrass you. Remember, whether you're a lady who expects to be wined and dined or one who believes in going Dutch, cheap isn't about how much money your guy has. It's a state of mind. Don't confuse cheap with poor. Poor originates in the wallet. Cheap comes from the heart. The cheap guy will always cling to his money like it's the last life preserver on the *Titanic* no matter how much of it he has, and the generous guy will always round the tip up, going down with the ship if he has to. The willingness to throw in an extra dollar when it's needed or buy a friend coffee or pick up a cab for another couple sharing with you at the end of a long night shows a generosity of spirit, a belief that it all evens out in the end. The guy who's always stingy with money may very well be stingy with other things. If he obsesses over the extra three bucks he threw in to make sure the waiter had a decent tip, what else will he obsess about? If he slyly doesn't throw in enough money when a bill comes, who knows what else he might fail to mention. You can rent a video when times are tough. You can serve a frozen dinner by candlelight. You can share one drink with four umbrellas in it, instead of having four glasses of five-year-old scotch. But all the money in the world won't make a cheap guy fun to be around. And all the cheap guys in the world won't kick in anything extra for happiness.

Younger Guys: When Minuses Are Pluses

If you're twenty-seven and you dismiss a guy as being too young because he's twenty-four, count your blessings and count your days. Before you know it, the Younger Guy will be ten years younger, and you'll be telling him you're only three years older. With any luck, he'll believe it. Love means never having to say you're forty. Younger guys are like your favorite pair of shoes: You spend too much money on them, but they make you feel fantastic and they look fucking great. They also don't have kids. If shoes could have flat abs, random make-outs, and hope, younger men would be obsolete.

When deciding whether or not to date younger men, consider first the pithy wisdom passed down by a wise friend: They die first. So why not hitch your wagon to a star that's not going to burn out way before you do? But younger men aren't ready to commit, to settle down, to have a baby, you say. Well, I'll ask you, how many of those "age-appropriate" guys you've been dating have settled down with you? I'm not suggesting you shouldn't know what you want and go after it. I'm just saying, keep an open mind. A younger man is a great way to jump-start your dating life, to revitalize, to remind yourself of why you're so great and why you should be out there, running amok. Remember leaving a bar at two A.M. and asking, "Where should we go next?" Remember being admired for what you're trying to do, rather than feeling judged for what you haven't achieved? Remember when you actually could remember things at all? Well, it's better the second time around when you seem super-cool because you have the confidence that only experience (age) can bring. In the words of one of the greatest bands of our time, Duran Duran, you have danced into the fire. And you have come back out of the fire and taken down your Duran Duran posters. Now you are ready to date guys who don't remember Duran Duran.

Seeing as men never really grow up, and seeing as men in their thirties still think the supermodel with the lobotomy who will date them is right around the corner, what have you got to lose? Don't take it all so seriously all the time. Do you need the baby this week? It's a no-harm, no-foul situation. They have years and years ahead of them to date, to fall in love, and to get heartbroken. So why not just try it? You tried Atkins, didn't you? And Bikram yoga. And kabbalah. And what if he turns out to be the kind of younger man a friend of mine ended up married to—the kind who told her on their second date he wanted kids and if she didn't, she shouldn't waste his time? Well, then you won the lottery . . . while eating a Snickers bar . . . in a hot tub. And if you don't want kids, then think of dating a younger man as your way of working with youth. One cocktail at a time.

Here's a quick overview of some of the younger men you might run into in your travels and where you might take them:

The Mensch:

So sweet you'll wish you had dental insurance. This guy is the best friend, the one likes to spend leisurely weekend afternoons nursing a Bloody Mary or five and talking about everything from what he's going to do with his life to what you're going to do with yours. He's like the younger brother you never had. Or a good replacement for the one you didn't get along with. This relationship may never turn into romance, but that way you can keep it.

Hope Springs Juvenile:

He's like a puppy dog, bouncing around your heels. This younger guy is full of "ideas," "opinions," and "plans." He has no idea that having them is useless, and that's cute! The things you once debated and long ago made up your mind about, he's just asking questions about. He even likes to dance (what?). Hey, maybe you're not as jaded as you like to think. Plus he thinks you're hot.

Leave Your Boyfriend For Me:

Ask yourself, why are you perfect for him if you're dating someone else? That's exactly why. But, you know, the attention is great. The disheveled "I can't sleep with the lights off" look?

Adorable. The complete intolerance of anyone who isn't you? Awesome. The self-loathing. Understandable. The end result: He'll go back to his ex-girlfriend from college. Hey, it was fun while it really didn't even exist.

Too Cool for School:
Then why did you go to Harvard, asshole? Next.

The Loner:
Sober. Silent. Self-sufficient. The good news is he owns a truck! The breakup is sure to happen in the streets, during a dramatic turn of events, over a petty jealousy or not chipping in for gas. But as you watch him manually shift into the sunset, at least you can be satisfied knowing he got off on baby talk.

Stone Cold Fox (SCF):
This guy is hot. No need to analyze. You can't fight this feeling anymore. And why should you?

Younger Guy Bonus Question

Your younger guy thinks the name Duran Duran comes from:

a The villain of the Roger Vadim film *Barbarella*, starring Ms. Jane Fonda

b An aerobics move from the Jane Fonda workout: And one, and two, Duran Duran

c The name of the house in *On Golden Pond*

d A Flock of Seagulls lyric

The Score

The correct answer is **a**—10 extra points! And an additional 10 extra points for dating a younger guy!

Younger guy bonus score: _____

Cumulative score: _____

PART TWO

Getting to Know You

The first bloom is off the rose or whatever that weird cliché is. Now is the time when you really get to know each other. The time when maybe you find another toothbrush in your toothbrush holder, and not just because you're too lazy to throw the old one away. When, if you didn't have too much to drink on that first date, you have sex for the first time—and the sixth. When the unthinkable happens: You meet his friends. He meets yours. This is a time full of discovery, full of happiness, and full of deal-breakers.

The getting-to-know-you stage is when you decide whether to strengthen the bond, to become boyfriend-girlfriend, to call each other adorable nicknames like "Poops O'Shea" and "Crazy Pants" and "You owe me twenty bucks, remember?" It may be that time when you take that first tentative step onto the yellow brick road of commitment, certain that a gleaming palace and the answer to your all your prayers is dead-ahead. Not to mention a Toto of your very own. (Dog or band, you decide.) But it's also a time when you might end up in a shadowy forest, full of creepy sounds and signs bearing the epithets NO FOREPLAY or ASIAN LETTERS TATTOO or EMOTIONAL ROBOT. Don't forget to look up at those signs once in a while, lest you lose your way for a period of time ranging from several months to several years. And watch out for flying monkeys.

CHAPTER 5

NO MORE SINGLE RED ROSES!

Romance

Once upon a time, a lady went on a blind date. Well, twice really, 'cause sometimes a lady must stumble a couple of times before she learns not to wear stilettos on cobblestone. She was heading for the restaurant when she noticed a guy who looked like he might be her date, standing to one side of the door, holding a bouquet of flowers. She walked swiftly into the restaurant and took a seat, hoping against hope that he wasn't her date. Then he appeared in the doorway. Then he sat at her table. Damn. A bouquet of flowers? On a blind date? Save your lira, Fabio. You don't know her. You don't know anything about her. What if her eyes start watering and she starts sneezing? What if she doesn't own a vase? What if she just doesn't give a shit about flowers 'cause all they do is die? What if she's a slob so flowers don't brighten up her home, but instead they clutter up her home? A lady's purse has a place for keys, a cell phone, and a tiny bottle of hand lotion, but you've yet to see the purse with a flower compartment. Must you walk around like some pageant winner all night? No, you have a choice. You can walk around like you just performed in *The Nutcracker* instead. And please, no more single red roses! What's that for, to hold in your teeth? Unless he's coming to see your flamenco performance, you probably won't be needing that.

A true romantic doesn't want to be bothered with someone giving lip service to romance. Giving lip service to romance sounds double romantic, almost dirty, but from here on out, we will refer to this lazy guy's shortcut as Fauxmance. Defined very simply, Fauxmance is buying you some junk women are supposed to like, as designated by movies we watch, celebrities we ogle, and advertisers who want us to spend our hard-earned cash. We've been hypnotized to buy into cookie-cutter Fauxmance, and the cookie cutters are shaped like Diamonds, Flowers, Chocolate, and Lingerie. And many women react to these things like Pavlov's dog caught in a belfry. But consider this: Anyone can go out and buy you something expensive if he has the money. Anyone who has the money can go out and hire someone to buy you something expensive. That's economic, not romantic. Romance comes from the heart. It's not about a purchase, it's about a gesture. Romance shouldn't be a transaction. Recently I overheard a woman talking about a "push gift" she had received. That's a gift bought for a woman who's had a baby. Is that romantic? It sounds like it's another checkmark on the list of items to store in the safety-deposit box in case your guy ever leaves you. Women talk about this gift like it's expected payment for having a baby with him—for him—despite him—to spite him? Ideally, wouldn't having a baby be something you want to do together, not something that wins you a prize if it hits the bull's-eye when it comes flying out of you? *Ding! And the lady wins a tennis bracelet from Tiffany!* Sure, nice things are nice. And ladies love to be spoiled. But I caution against mistaking retail for romance. Because, frankly, mistaking retail for romance makes you a big whore.

You may be hard to buy for. You may be super picky and know exactly what you want, and it may be a nightmare for your guy. That's when he needs to get a little creative. One year, around the time of my birthday, all the lights in my house burned out. I'm short and it's a pain to stand on a chair and the lightbulbs over the bathroom mirror are funky and I don't understand them. (Shorthand: I'm a girl. Giggle, hair toss, aaaand scene.) I offhandedly mentioned the situation to my boyfriend. I came home after being out late, in the wee hours of the morning of my birthday, switched on the hall light and settled down on my couch to watch some relaxing television, which, along with a can of Pringles and the alcohol consumed that night, would lull me into much-needed sleep. It took me a minute to realize that even though my hall light wasn't working, I had just turned it on. Wait a *minute* . . . I then went through my apartment happily turning on and off all the lights that had previously burned out. My boyfriend had come over when I wasn't home and fixed them so they would be working when I got home on my birthday.

Romance takes time. Romance takes thoughtfulness. Sometimes, and this is the tricky one, it takes taste. But mostly it takes attentiveness. Does he notice when you say you like something you see in a window? Does he remember what movie makes you cry? Does he know what kind of taste you have in music and books? Does he know the silly joke that brings you to tears? When you offhandedly mention something you need, or point it out deliberately fifty times, does he listen and remember? Is he willing to do a little sneaky spying? Does he have your best friend's number in his cell, so when he's stumped or he forgets, he has a consultant on call with your best interests in mind? Does he care enough to take the extra fifteen minutes that make the difference between a nice gift and a romantic gesture?

But hey, if you're completely unswayed and you still think no matter what, diamonds are a girl's best friend, my wish for you is that they're Harry Winston and not Zales. Best of luck with that.

The Quiz: As Time Goes Buy

1. Your birthday is coming up! He:

    a Gathers a few friends together for a nice dinner

    b Looks at my license to figure out when it is after I drop major hints

    c Plans a blowout surprise party

    d Has no clue

2. For a birthday gift you get:

    a A gift certificate to my favorite clothing store

    b A gift certificate to his favorite sporting-goods store

    c A sheepish smile and an excuse

    d That treat-myself gift I've been saving up to buy for months

3. Your gift is wrapped in:

    a The bag it came in

    b Photocopied newspaper stories from the day I was born

    c The paper I wrapped *his* last gift in

    d The paper the nice lady at the store wrapped it in

4. What kind of birthday cake do you get?

a Entenmann's—still in the box

b A nice bakery cake with all the trimmings

c A cake that he makes out of Krispy Kremes—they're my favorite

d None: "You're off carbs, remember?"

5. He's broke on your birthday. He:

a Runs me a bubble bath, lights some candles, cracks open a bottle of cheap wine

b Doesn't come home till late

c Makes me a mixed CD of songs that are all about how he feels about me

d Says next year we'll do something great

6. Your birthday card:

a Is something my mother would like; it's super-corny and not me at all

b Has a photo on the front and a heartfelt note on the inside

c Doesn't exist—he scrawls my name on the box the gift comes in

d Handmade and hilarious

7. It's Valentine's Day:

a It's a big box of heart-shaped candy with ruffles on the front

b Any excuse to go to dinner together is a welcome one!

c He doesn't believe in a consumer-created holiday; it's all bullshit

d He takes me on a tour around town of the first weeks of our relationship, ending at the place we had our first date

8. You love flowers. He:

a Loves kung fu films

b Makes a window box of my favorites for my bedroom so I'll see them when I wake up

c Grabs the first flowers he sees at the deli

d Handpicks a bouquet for me

9. When do you get gifts?

a When he's done something wrong and he doesn't want to talk about it

b On special occasions

c When I remind him a gift-appropriate occasion is coming up

d Whenever he sees something that he thinks I would like, no matter how silly or little

10. Your guy's idea of a great gift is:

a Whatever looks OK at the first store he walks into; he can't stand shopping

b Something extravagant I absolutely don't need but would love, like cool earrings or funky sunglasses

c Trashy lingerie—I have a drawer full of it!

d A scale

11. The two of you are watching a romantic film. He:

a Keeps flipping to ESPN

b Brings a box of Kleenex for me

c Laughs a little too loud . . . during the romantic scenes

d Falls asleep

12. It's your anniversary:

a He doesn't really know when our anniversary is; he doesn't keep track

b We don't really know when our anniversary is; we don't keep track

c We celebrate our yearly anniversary by doing something fun and new we both want to try, like taking ballroom dance lessons or going camping

d We celebrate our anniversary every month!

13. You've planned a romantic evening, made dinner by candlelight, and you're all dressed up and looking hot. He had a shitty day:

a He's grumpy and I have to make him feel better

b He gets drunk, falls asleep fully dressed on top of the covers, and I have to undress him and put him to bed

c He tells me I look amazing and this is the best thing that's happened to him all day

d He tells me he needs to run out to the store for contact lens solution, but comes back with my favorite ice cream for dessert

14. The first time he says "I love you":

a Um . . . I should just know he feels that way

b He does it spontaneously because of some little thing I do

c It's only because I say it to him

d He puts thought into it and makes it a special night just to tell me

15. You tell him you're concerned the romance is going out of your relationship. He suggests:

a We both clear our calendars for the next weekend and spend it together catching up

b I take fifty dollars out of his wallet and "buy myself something pretty"

c Couples therapy

d I take a cardio strip class

1. **a** 3, **b** 2, **c** 4, **d** 1
2. **a** 3, **b** 2, **c** 1, **d** 4
3. **a** 1, **b** 4, **c** 2, **d** 3
4. **a** 2, **b** 3, **c** 4, **d** 1
5. **a** 3, **b** 1, **c** 4, **d** 2
6. **a** 2, **b** 3, **c** 1, **d** 4
7. **a** 3, **b** 2, **c** 1, **d** 4
8. **a** 1, **b** 4, **c** 2, **d** 3
9. **a** 1, **b** 3, **c** 2, **d** 4
10. **a** 2, **b** 4, **c** 3, **d** 1
11. **a** 3, **b** 4, **c** 2, **d** 1
12. **a** 1, **b** 2, **c** 4, **d** 3
13. **a** 2, **b** 1, **c** 3, **d** 4
14. **a** 1, **b** 3, **c** 2, **d** 4
15. **a** 4, **b** 2, **c** 3, **d** 1

50–60: Cupid, draw back your bow.

He's at the top of his romance game. He's thoughtful, he takes time to do special things for you, he knows what you like, he's imaginative, he's . . . imaginary. You have an imaginary boyfriend, admit it! This is the George Glass to your Jan Brady. I mean, I totally made this guy up. I didn't really think he was out there. Are you telling me he's out there? And you have him? Well, you showed me. Your work is done.

38-49: I feel for you, I *think* I love you.

While he's not Valentino, this guy is still really trying. Sometimes he gets it right, sometimes not so much. He may not always go out of his way with the big romantic gesture, but he cares and he often comes through, so you can forgive those few times when he doesn't love the tear-jerker you rented or doesn't wrap the gift himself. Look at all the great stuff he does!

26-37: Up a lazy river.

OK, seriously, this guy needs to step it up a little. He just wants to squeak by with little effort and lots of excuses. He doesn't quite remember things, and everything happens last minute and often because you force his hand. I'm not saying locked deep inside him somewhere there might not be a heart of gold, I'm just saying at the moment it's looking a bit tarnished.

15-25: But you don't know me.

Has he ever met you? Is he your prison pen pal? This guy never comes through. Every single time it's a lame excuse, or worse, no excuse at all. Why is he even in a relationship? Does he need a couch to crash on? Not good enough, lady. You deserve better. Get rid of him and buy yourself a congratulatory gift.

*Question exception: If you're doing that whole "celebrate our anniversary every month" thing and you've been dating for more than a month, no points off, but calm down. Nobody likes that.

Getting the Final Word In

The British are coming! The British are coming!! At least that's what you think until you're trapped under one of them thirteen pints later, and he's snoring.

Traitor! This is blasphemy! British guys are dreamy. They're so smart and witty. And they're so cool in their sharp suits and hip clothes. They're always so romantic. Even the cads are charming. They're like princes, but real princes, because over there, they still have princes. They're dashing. Look at all the British stars—Jude Law, Colin Firth, Clive Owen, Ewan McGregor (Scottish counts, right?). Chariots of fire, they're hot! Help, I'm swooning . . . but before I faint, one more thing—they have that amazing accent. It makes everything sound better. Even "it's malignant" sounds good when a British guy says it.

Just for fun, let's examine a purely hypothetical scenario involving you and a charming British rake. We'll call it "Your Name Here and British Guy: A Bawdy Tale of International Romance." You meet this British guy, oh, I don't know, let's say in Paris (ding, ding, ding, the board is completely lit up—it's Quadruple Romance Points!). He says things like "you're gorgeous" and "you're brilliant." Finally someone sees that you are gorgeous and brilliant. The British really are smarter than Americans. You don't understand yet that they say that about everyone. It's not like in the States where being gorgeous means you're very beautiful, and we have other descriptive words like cute and pretty and sexy. Where brilliant can't be equally applied to Albert Einstein and the fact that while you were at the store you picked up more Hob Nobs. No. They use these words universally, the way we might use "Hey asshole, move," or "Shut the fuck up." Like that.

Anyway, you meet British Guy, you spend days flirting, and then on your last night in Paris, you walk through the streets hand in hand. You spend a romantic night together, and the next day he must return to London. Oh well, you'll always have Paris! But against all odds, you manage to keep in touch, and you decide to fly to London to visit him. It's July and the ticket is really expensive, but who cares? I mean, this is so romantic. The most romantic thing that's ever happened in your life. Everyone you tell the story to can't believe how romantic this is. Caution, and hundreds of American dollars, are thrown to the wind. Then, two weeks before you're set to arrive, you and your nonrefundable ticket get an e-mail (not a call, mind you, an e-mail) informing you he got back together with his ex-girlfriend. Hmmm. That's not romantic. At least not for you.

Heed the moral of "Your Name Here and British Guy: A Bawdy Tale of International Romance," lest you, too, be drawn into the trap. Charming they may be, but they're still guys. Guys who can be incredible disappointments. Don't hang out in pubs hoping to meet them. Don't become a haberdasher. Don't take in a rugby match, for God's sake! OK. Admit it. No matter how bad that story is, no matter how sound the advice to steer clear of the British guy might be, you'd do it all again in a heartbeat, wouldn't you? All to hear that goddamn fakey accent one more time. Brilliant. Really fucking brilliant.

Whatcha Whatcha Whatcha Want:
A Gift Guide for Hapless Men

Punk-rock girl	He buys you *The Decline of Western Civilization* and gets Penelope Spheeris to autograph it. He writes a song for you entitled "I Love the Way You Hate Everyone."
Heavy-metal chick	He finds an original *Appetite for Destruction* T-shirt and bids for it successfully on eBay. He has your pit bull, Lita Ford, carry it out to you when your band is practicing in the garage.
High-powered exec	Leather portfolio with matching leather whip.
Performer	He comes and watches your shows and no matter what happens, he says, "You were fantastic!!" Did you hear that? Four people in the audience, sound problems, breakdown on stage . . . Fanastic!
Artist	He creates a show of your work at his place and sends out invites to all your friends for the opening party.
Performance artist	A yam.
Girly girl	He buys you an evening bag, the kind that you can fit one lipstick and a cell phone in. In the bag is a jewelry box and a cell phone. In the jewelry box is a note that says "Call me. I'm yours." You open up the cell phone and there's one number in it. You call. A mysterious man picks up and gives you an address. You go to the

	address. It's Tiffany. Your boyfriend takes you up to the counter and a sales person hands him a ring. And right there in front of your cat and everyone, he proposes to you.
Athlete	He enters you both in a marathon and you train and run together.
Activist	He lays down on a city street in protest with you. It doesn't matter what you're protesting, the guy is risking hepatitis, for God's sake.
Scholar	He learns Telugu so he can read your thesis in the original language.

Chapter 6

The Land Down Under

Sex

Sex is a topic that's almost staggeringly wide open (get it, nudge, nudge). To cover it all, one would have to possess Dr. Ruth–like powers and one mean German accent. Think of all the crazy things people like to do. Some people like dressing up as babies or being saddled and ridden like horses or sleeping with

Republicans. If we're being honest, and I hope we are, very few people's sexuality is completely straight ahead, lacking in any kind of dark side or perversity. Seriously, how could you stay in one position all the time? If nothing else, you cramp up. So we do a little role-play or talk dirty in bed or have sex in a park. Then it's no surprise that having sex can be like opening Pandora's box, and finding everything from a guy who just looooves to spank you to a guy who wants you to pee on him in a kiddie pool—and all the colors of the rainbow in between. And there are a lot of colors in that rainbow.

Some guys have no idea what they're doing in bed. They charge ahead like they're running with the bulls in Pamplona and stopping to admire the scenery will get them trampled. Ironically, you are the one who ends up feeling trampled. It's the sexual equivalent of being passed the relay baton. Is there a finish line on the headboard that you're unaware of? These ultra goal-oriented guys have a list, and every bullet point on that list has to do with their pleasure. Is this a permanent, inflexible state of mind or do they just not know any better? Knowing which is true for your guy can make all the difference in deciding how to approach the issue and whether it's even possible to make any headway (if you'll excuse the expression, nudge, nudge). After all, learning how to please a woman is a bit like playing video games your entire life and then being asked to build a ship in a bottle. It's a delicate, detail-oriented process that takes a lot of practice and attention. And they're used to blowing shit up. With a joystick (if you catch my meaning, nudge, nudge).

For some guys, however, it's a point of pride to make sure *you* have a good time in bed, too. With one of these guys you'll never suddenly hear snoring from the other side of the bed when you thought it was "your turn." On the contrary, they understand that your body encompasses everything from the top of your head to your feet, not just a few key tourist attractions. These guys actually enjoy the experience of sex, the fact that it involves two people and there's something more in it for them (and you) than an orgasm. These guys may just be great guys who went to a lot of summer camp, but then again you might want to think twice from now on before ruling out a guy for being too short . . . After all, if he's got something to prove, his proving ground just might be the sack.

No matter what you and your guy are into, what's most important is that your guy knows what your limits, boundaries, and safe words are, and really knows what excites you. (And for those of you who, just like in the romance chapter, are saying "diamonds" right now . . . seriously, look within. Never too late to grow.)

The Quiz: (Please Sing) Oooo-oo-oo-oo-oo-oo, I Wanna Sex You Up

1. You know he wants to have sex when:

   a He comes home with an unexpected gift

   b He gets a certain mischievous look in his eyes

   c He says, "Wanna do it?"

   d He's dressed up as Robin Hood

2. A surefire way to get him excited is:

a Read the *Wall Street Journal* aloud

b Technically correct knots, as outlined in his old Boy Scout handbook

c Let him watch ESPN

d Touch him anywhere; he's a guy, after all

3. The first thing he does in the bedroom is:

a Check his BlackBerry; someone from work might be trying to reach him

b Jump on me and pull me into bed

c Make sure there's no light whatsoever in the room

d Take out his silk scarves

e Put on a Breathe Right strip

4. His kisses remind you:

a Of a treasure hunt; why else would he be digging around like that with his tongue?

b Of why I'm having sex with him in the first place

c Of your place, slave

d Of relatives at family holidays. Ewwwww

5. When it comes to foreplay:

a They should call it fiveplay, my guy is so conscientious about it

b It doesn't; it's all business and apparently he's billing by the minute

c It's like precision cheerleading, the routine is so predictable

d He mixes it up so much he could be a bartender

6. To get naked he:

a Doesn't—he always leaves his T-shirt and socks on

b Painstakingly and meticulously removes every item of his clothing and folds it neatly

c Lets me pull his clothes off in the heat of the moment

d Does something he refers to as the Dance of Dionysus—does anyone know how to get red wine stains out of sheets?

7. To get you naked he:

a Liquors me up

b Puts a twenty in my underwear

c Undresses me

d Says, "your turn," while looking away

8. **When you're naked in front of him he makes you feel:**

   a Great, by reminding me of all the things he likes about my body

   b Like he might be legally blind and has never told me

   c Like a Goddess who gets to eat cookies

   d Like I should call Jenny Craig

9. **You're ready to have sex when you realize you don't have any condoms. He:**

   a Is relieved because he can't have sex with a condom; it doesn't feel good

   b Says no big deal, there's plenty to do without having intercourse

   c Runs out and buys some immediately

   d Says, "Oh well, how about a game of chess? You play, right?"

10. **His favorite position is:**

    a Any one in which I do all the work

    b Eyes closed

    c Stretched out on the rack

    d Less federal government, more states' rights, free markets, and civil liberties

    e Whatever works best for both of us at the moment

1 1. While you're having sex with him you think of:

a Papa Smurf—is that weird?

b Nothing, I'm totally in the moment

c Pudding, and I don't even like pudding

d Exactly where my life went wrong

1 2. You know he reached orgasm because:

a He yells, "Yeah! That's what I'm talking about!" like always

b He's snoring

c He unzips the hood to get some air

d He's vocal during it and affectionate after it

e He suddenly stops moving and excuses himself to use the bathroom

1 3. When you're finished having sex he:

a Immediately falls asleep on his side of the bed

b Spoons me and stays up talking with me

c Takes off his rubber gloves

d Leaves; he can't sleep in the same bed with someone else

14. Shit, the condom breaks . . . he:

a Freaks out, yelling, "You're not keeping it, right?"

b Says, "No big deal, it's not like I have anything that I know of"

c Helps me figure out how to get the morning-after pill the morning after

d Says, "Not again, I cannot afford this"

e Showers like he's in *Silkwood*

15. The place you most often have sex is:

a Bathrooms in bars

b There's other places besides bed?

c At swingers conventions

d Wherever we happen to be in the house when the mood strikes us

e Wherever we happen to be when he's horny

16. The frequency with which you have sex is:

a I don't keep track; we're both happy with it

b Staggering, I'm literally staggering

c Every six months, like the equinox

d Whenever his team wins

17. If you say you're not in the mood for sex, he:

a Says, "Let's just go watch someone else do it, then"

b Says, "Phew! I was hoping you were going to say that!" while laughing nervously

c Says, "Wow, your friend Christina said this would happen"

d Asks if there's anything he can do to get me in the mood

18. You were looking forward to having sex and you just got your period:

a Doesn't matter

b He whines, "Why does this happen every month?"

c He worships my woman's strength

d He's excited—can't get pregnant tonight, so no condom, right??

19. You're both really drunk:

a We're really horny, he passes out

b We have fun, wild sex

c We're in the middle of it, he passes out cold

d We have wild, crazy, best-sex-ever sex and then neither of us can remember it

20. When he doesn't feel like having sex, he:

a Lets me know why so I won't feel like it's about me

b Fakes a hernia

c Fakes being asleep

d Really *is* asleep

21. The song that he puts on to get in the mood is:

a "You Can't Always Get What You Want"

b "We Don't Have to Take Our Clothes Off"

c "Hurts So Good"

d "Our" song

22. When he's getting a little dirty, he:

a Likes to be submissive to me

b Spanks me

c Takes out the *Kama Sutra*

d Tries to get me interested in a threesome for the three-millionth time

23. He asks you to do something you're not really comfortable with:

a He understands, and we talk about it later

b "You're so constrained by society!"

c "You never care about what I want!"

d I wish he would . . .

24. Your favorite sex game is:

a George Bush and Condoleeza Rice

a Two people who feel weird about playing games and crack up in the middle

c Guy who really likes blow jobs and girl who gives them

d "Why Can't We Just Have Normal Sex?" quiz hour

The Score:

1. **a** 2, **b** 4, **c** 1, **d** 3
2. **a** 2, **b** 3, **c** 1, **d** 4
3. **a** 1, **b** 4, **c** 2, **d** 3, **e** 2
4. **a** 1, **b** 4, **c** 3, **d** 2
5. **a** 4, **b** 1, **c** 2, **d** 3
6. **a** 1, **b** 2, **c** 4, **d** 3
7. **a** 1, **b** 3, **c** 4, **d** 2

8. a 4, b 2, c 3, d 1

9. a 1, b 3, c 4, d 2

10. a 1, b 2, c 3, d 2, e 4

11. a 3, b 4, c 2, d 1

12. a 1, b 1, c 3, d 4, e 2

13. a 2, b 4, c 3, d 1

14. a 1, b 3, c 4, d 1, e 2

15. a 3, b 2, c 3, d 4, e 1

16. a 4, b 3, c 2, d 1

17. a 3, b 2, c 1, d 4

18. a 4, b 2, c 3, d 1

19. a 2, b 4, c 1, d 3

20. a 4, b 1, c 2, d 3

21. a 1, b 2, c 3, d 4

22. a 2, b 4, c 3, d 1

23. a 4, b 3, c 1, d 2

24. a 2, b 4, c 1, d 3

78–96: Mr. Lover Man.

What was it we said about sex? Ah, yes. It should be about mutual enjoyment. And so it is. Shaba.

60–77: Super Freak.

If this is what you're into, OK. But isn't it all going to get a little tired, like a Broadway show you've seen over and over again, with its big, glitzy numbers and its elaborate costumes and its long wait for the bathroom during intermission? While experimentation can be exciting and fun and turn a sexual side of Uncle Ben's white rice into Zatarain's, just be cognizant of the guy who *has* to go to the extreme to get off. Because one day you might want to just have plain old sex again.

42–59: Too shy shy.

You can't *really* leave your hat on. Come on. How did you ever have sex with this guy in the first place? There are some major issues here that I think you cannot solve no matter how much you like him. Bring in the professionals—no, I don't mean the hookers. I think he has a little work to do in the loosening-up department. If you find yourself in the missionary position that often, you better be traveling to foreign countries to help the poor.

24–41: I bet you think this sex is about you.

He's going to push your head down. Push him out the door.

Chapter 6 score: _____

Cumulative score: _____

Getting the Last Word In

A star is porn. It used to be that sex was everywhere we looked. Well, now that sex is hardcore. Whether you think it's right or not, it's always right there. It's a fact of our modern world, with its pay television, video rentals, and Internet access, that porn has become mainstream. Traci Lords stars in legit films, porn stars are the subjects of coffee table photography books, and Ron Jeremy is as much of a household name as Ronald McDonald. When it comes to the question of whether your guy has partaken or will at some point partake of pornography, live by this simple rhyme: Unless your guy is born-again, he's going to be watching porn again. No matter your personal inclinations, possible moral objections, or irrational feelings of jealousy, watching porn for the straight man is like going to Broadway musicals for the gay man. And like watching porn for the gay man. You don't have to take it lying down, as it were, but you do have to be realistic about it. It is going to show up under your bed or in a sock drawer.

The main thing to remember is it's not about you. It's not about something you're not doing or some way in which you're lacking. It's complete and utter fantasy. If your guy wanted to date a bimbo with a boob job who gave head to every guy who delivered a pizza to her, or every detective trying to solve the Case of the Missing Dildo or every Captain of the Starship Enterguys that landed on Planet Threesome, he'd date that kind of girl. But he's dating you because, in addition to having sex, he enjoys conversing and visiting his parents. The women in porn movies are actors, and as talented as

they may be, they're still playing a role. So don't inter-
nalize it, just leave it where it is—in the living room
when you're not home. (Chances are you're reading this
wondering if he knows where your stash is . . .) And if
you really can't bear the idea that your guy might need
any stimulation other than you, then get prepared to
look long and hard (if you will, nudge, nudge) for a guy
who never indulges in it. Some of them are probably out
there, too. The ones that left the seminary.

What Not to Hear in Bed

I know my kisses are like poison.
> *They must be. My sex drive just died.*

Mmmm. Yummy.
> *Ewww. Gross.*

Get ready for "the treatment"!
> *I'm not sure my insurance covers this, Dr. Love.*

You make me come!
> *Thanks, Master of the Obvious.*

Christina! Christina!!!
> *My name's Jane.*

You're my queen.
> *I hereby sentence you to death.*

Who's your daddy?
> *Dr. Mal Rosenthal, DDS . . . Why, do you need bridge work?*

I'm done.
> *Yes, yes you are.*

You want me to *what?*
> *Let's start with being a better listener.*

Spit on me.
> *Get off me.*

What are you going to do with all that ass?
> *I don't know. What are you going to do with all your time alone?*

Someone's been a naughty girl.
> *OK, OK, I'll put the money back in your wallet . . .*

I want to make you hate me.
> *Done and done.*

CHAPTER 7

ABOVE AND BELOW
THE BELT

 Abs, Penis, & Feet

Now that you've had sex, the clothes come off, and so do the gloves. You might be surprised by what you find under all that army-surplus camouflage he's been using to such great advantage. Is his skin a bit rough around the extremities? Wow . . . a tattoo . . . of the masks of comedy and tragedy, no less! And his feet. If you wanted to see something that horrifying, you'd go to a slasher movie.

It's a world of wonder—wonder how he gets away with it. You practically dip your entire body in a vat of cream and swaddle yourself in plastic wrap each night to stay silky smooth. You pay to have your nails cut, buffed, and polished, your calluses smoothed. Someone spreads hot wax on various, highly sensitive parts of your body and *rips* out your hair with pieces of fabric. The slightest sign of weight gain is the subject of a Gettysburg Address–like phone conversation with your best friend and anyone else who will listen. And is there really a cure for cellulite, because your overflowing medicine cabinet can't hold any more products and you can't handle any more disappointment. Your butt is too big, breasts are too small, you wish you had longer legs, your feet are so wide, your hands look masculine, is that a spider vein, your skin tone is uneven, and why isn't your hair shiny??? Meanwhile, he has not cut his toenails in seven years. And don't get me started on fungus.

How can it be that with legs that look like he runs, and not just away from creditors, and muscular arms he maintains with the occasional living-room push-up session, he still has a little poochy stomach? How did he achieve an illusion worthy of Doug Henning and seem in shape this whole time, only to pull a gut out of his hat at the last minute? When you put on weight you just get a bit curvier. You are the inspiration for entire artistic movements. Sure, you're not an expert on art, but you can't seem to recall Cézanne's Beer Belly series. Why does all his excess weight have to settle in one place? Is he going to use it later? Is this a step in the evolutionary process, wherein someday men will feed our children using nutrients stored in their stomachs? Can't guys get a six-pack by doing six sit-ups? Can't they get a washboard stomach just by carrying the wash up a flight of stairs?

And let's weigh in, as it were, on his penis. Size matters. Oops, did I say that out loud? Sorry to your fella if he's not endowed like Harvard Business School, but I've never once yet heard any woman exclaim with delight, "Oh, and he's tiny!" Yes, the vagina has all these nerve endings, blah, blah, blah, and there's someone for everyone, blah-dee-blee, but frankly, the only time I want to say "Is it in?" is when I'm playing an intern on *ER*, trying to perform a made-for-TV intubation. The only time women say size doesn't matter is when they haven't had size. It's like fake Fendi. The only time you like it is when you haven't had the real thing. You think it's great, and then you feel a real Fendi bag, and there's a kind of heft to it. And then you realize what you've been missing out on. Suddenly, yours doesn't seem so nice anymore. Look, it's not like he needs to be *huge,* but if he's too small, it's just not going to work. Maybe we need a measure at our bedsides like they have at traveling carnivals: Any penis smaller than this cannot go on this ride.

Your love for him may be tested when the trappings of polite society are literally thrown aside and you are faced with the literal naked truth. Did you know his nipples were pierced and a chain connects them? Does he really have a barbed-wire tattoo? Didn't Pamela Anderson corner that market in that film . . . what was it called? . . . oh, *Barb Wire*. When the Levis drop to the floor, does he have Lady Butt and the lesser-known affliction, Lady Legs? Oh no, not track marks again.

The Quiz: Grin and Bare It

1. His eyebrows:

   a I'm dating Peter Gallagher!

   b They get out of hand, he gets scissors in hand

   c He has two of them?

2. His skin:

   a Hard-boiled

   b Baby soft

   c Things that go bumpy in the night

3. His skin tone:

   a Holy mole-y!

   b Oompa Loompa

   c Even Steven

4. His elbows:

   a Sandpaper

   b So smooth, I don't quite trust them

   c If he's a frog, that means he's a prince, too, right?

5. His hands:

a *On the Waterfront*

b *The Crying Game*

c *I Was a Teenage Werewolf*

6. His fingernails:

a He must be really hungry

b He must be really lazy

c He must not want to snag me

7. His chest:

a Brack

b Archie

c Superman

8. His nipples:

a Quarters

b Nickels

c Dimes

9. His back:

   a Luke Skywalker

   b Yoda

   c Chewbacca

10. His stomach:

   a He has a six-pack

   b He drank a six-pack

   c He can rest a six-pack on top of it

11. His ass:

   a Maybe if he got off it once in a while . . .

   b Hard as a rock, and cute as two buttons

   c Dude looks like a lady

12. Hey, Goldilocks, what's his penis like?

   a This one is too big

   b This one is too little

   c This one is just right

13. His legs:

   a Rocky Balboa

   b Bullwinkle Moose

   c Magilla Gorilla

14. His feet:

  a Prickly like a cactus

  b Cracked like a dried-out riverbed

  c Soft as a rose petal

15. His toenails:

  a Domesticated

  b Three-toed sloth

  c Great-grandpa

16. His worst tattoo:

  a Raggedy Ann

  b Naked Betty Boop

  c Hervé Villechaize on *Fantasy Island* reruns

17. His tattoo coverage:

  a I'm with the band

  b I will dare

  c You'll never work in this town again

18. What a surprise!

  a Fingerprints around his neck

  b Body right out of a Prince video

  c Prince Albert

19. He smells like:

a Germany—I'm always in the middle of cologne

b Freshly showered guy

c Wet dog

The Score

1. **a** 2, **b** 3, **c** 1
2. **a** 1, **b** 3, **c** 2
3. **a** 1, **b** 2, **c** 3
4. **a** 1, **b** 3, **c** 2
5. **a** 2, **b** 3, **c** 1
6. **a** 1, **b** 2, **c** 3
7. **a** 1, **b** 2, **c** 3
8. **a** 1, **b** 2, **c** 3
9. **a** 3, **b** 2, **c** 1
10. **a** 3, **b** 2, **c** 1
11. **a** 1, **b** 3, **c** 2
12. **a** 2, **b** 1, **c** 3
13. **a** 3, **b** 2, **c** 1
14. **a** 1, **b** 2, **c** 3
15. **a** 3, **b** 1, **c** 2
16. **a** 2, **b** 1, **c** 3

17. **a** 2, **b** 3, **c** 1

18. **a** 2, **b** 3, **c** 1

19. **a** 2, **b** 3, **c** 1

45–57: Caretaker.
Uses lotion. Showers regularly. Keeps himself fit. Check and mate.

32–44: Take care.
OK, he'll let it slide a little. Maybe he forgets his eyebrows are out of control or that you can see his tattoo. But he's serviceable and hopefully salvageable. Just keep an eye on his toenails.

19–31: Cares not.
I just hope you guys live on a commune.

Chapter 7 score: _____

Cumulative score: _____

Getting the Last Word In

OK, that's it. We're going to draw a line. We're drawing the line at describing fat men as "sexy." Let's just all agree the charade ends here and breathe a huge sigh of relief, a sigh that will be heard 'round the world because we've been practicing our breathing every week in Pilates. I know, I know. We're women. What's so great about us is that we see past the purely superficial, the external.

When considering what makes a guy sexy, we don't just look at physique. We take into account talent and sense of humor and that aphrodisiac to trump all aphrodisiacs, power. We're so wonderfully enlightened. If only we were enlightened enough to demand equal treatment. How many times have you heard a guy describe an overweight woman as sexy because she made him laugh? Why is Oprah's weight the topic of countless conversations and media profiles? Kirstie Alley had to make her weight the focus of her career to keep her career going. That makes her sassy, sure, but not sexy.

There's no need to attack any men personally. We're still above that. Besides, the list is way too long. Just watch any television show, any film, open any magazine and you can see countless examples of the overweight guy being dubbed a sexy superstar with the woman who looks like she lives on a diet of lettuce, water, and the occasional does of flaxseed oil. Stay strong and stick to the pact. If you must give a chubby guy a compliment, use the word my friends and I use, *chexy*. But stop getting weak in the knees for men whose knees are weak because they can't support their own weight anymore. And if you find your will failing, think of this. If you have said something negative about your weight even once this week, if you have deprived yourself of something you really wanted to eat, if you have taken a spin class, if you have felt a twinge of jealousy at seeing a thinner woman walk down the street, you are not allowed to give an inch, as it were, to a chubby guy. You can call him smart, talented, witty, rich, and powerful. Just not sexy.

Metrosexual: Man or Myth

The Metrosexual. Much has been written about him, and yet an air of mystery surrounds him. Is he indeed out there, buying nice clothes and using more than one hair product? Do we dare to believe his legend, the songs that tell of his exploits at Barneys and the trendy restaurants and bars of newly gentrified neighborhoods? The epic poems that speak of his sensitivity, his romantic nature. Oh, sing, sing of the Metrosexual, come to save women from the Guy's Guy. Sing of his skin, smooth as, well, ours. Sing of his taking longer to get ready for a date than we do. Sing of his . . . singing.

The Metrosexual has been defined variously as a straight man who finally has to put up with all the insane and sadistic grooming rituals that women have always had to endure, a straight man who delights in finally being able to fully flaunt his vanity, and a man whose sexuality is ultimately irrelevant because he is only capable of loving himself. And that, as they say, is the rub. The only difference is that the rub in this case is performed with a moisturizing cleansing lotion with tiny exfoliating beads. Wouldn't it just be like a straight guy that when he has finally evolved, along with the help of advertisers, glossy men's magazines, and *Queer Eye for the Straight Guy*, into a guy who has a skin regimen, wears designer clothing, and isn't afraid to cry, he still has no time for us because he's too busy admiring himself? Instead of looking over your shoulder at the sports bar to check the scores of whatever game is on the big screen TV, he's looking behind you at the giant mirror on the wall of the bistro you're in to check his hair. And when he cries, he takes off his suede jacket first. Suede stains easily.

Yes, the Metrosexual exists. But sadly, only for himself.

CHAPTER 8

THE ULTIMATE TEST

 *Friends*

You've seen it time and time again: The amazing, accomplished, attractive woman who's fun to be around and could have her pick of guys, but somehow ends up with the guy who not only has no interest in her friends, but actively discourages her from seeing them. Kaaaaa-zam! Suddenly, she disappears. All these years she seemed cool, and then this one guy comes along and you feel like you never knew her at all. Why has she forsaken her friends? Maybe she takes so much distance from them because she fears the inevitable. If she talks to her friends like she used to, they'll tell her what she already knows deep down in her heart: Her boyfriend is an asshole. Your friends are your friends for a reason. And no guy worth his Calvin Klein boxer briefs would ever encourage you to feel any other way. No guy is so magical that he's worth your turning into the Disappearing Friend. No one likes that trick.

It can be a delicate business, combining guy and friends. But if you are going to move forward with your guy, it's a must-do. It doesn't have to be done all the time. Here's a crazy idea—you both need your own lives and identities, and your friends have their own relationships with you that didn't always involve your guy. However, if for no other reason than delegating your dwindling free time, these two parties will have to go to parties together. Your guy is going to have to show an interest in your friends. If your guy acts like a sour, petulant child who needs all your attention when your friends are around, if he always makes an excuse to not spend time with them, he's simply not a keeper. Nor are your friends just some kind of insurance policy against future loneliness. They are the people who were there for you before he showed up to make everything perfect. He should be eager to connect with people who know so much about you and like you as much as he does. Why would your guy be threatened by your friends? In the absence of a rap sheet that sounds like dialogue from *NYPD Blue*, if they make you happy, that should make him happy. And let's face it, no matter what score he got in chapter 1, he's never going to like shopping with you.

And what about his friends? First and foremost, he should have some. The brooding, loner guy, who hitch-hikes from town to town, so troubled only a woman's touch can soothe his turbulent soul . . . save it for Court TV. A guy who has no friends is highly suspect, so much so he may end up a suspect when you go missing. A guy who has no friends will potentially lean too hard on you, demanding too much of your time. Remember, you're looking for a partner, not a child. Besides, his friends can supply you with important information. They reflect his taste and potentially reveal things previously not evident to you. Do they comment lewdly about other women? Do they engage in intellectual discussions? Do his friends make you feel like the "little lady," only there to bring a beer in from the fridge? Is that OK with him? Can you stand to have his friends around for years to come? And what about that one friend of his who gets a little too drunk and hits on you? Is your guy the type who collects oddball friends for fun? Do you really relish discussing what it's like to be national Scrabble champ because your guy thinks it's really cool?

Then there's the question of your guy having female friends. Though why this is a question, I've never been sure. Listen, Princess, unless you've really grown your hair out, no one's gonna be visiting you in that ivory tower of yours. Your guy should live in the real world. He should have female friends. There is something decidedly creepy or completely socially dysfunctional about a guy who doesn't know how to be friends with women. Or worse, who doesn't think women make good friends. Why would you even be attracted to that guy? Aren't you, at the bottom of it all, supposed to be his friend?

The Quiz: Keep Smiling, Keep Shining

1. **You're all hanging out watching *Grease,* and he unexpectedly shows up:**

   a My friends immediately make room for him on the couch and he joins in singing "Greased Lightning"

   b He puts the snacks he brought on the coffee table and takes drink orders

   c He interrupts the movie to make fun of it

   d He ignores the proceedings and disappears into the bedroom to read a book

   e He says hello to everyone, but doesn't join in; it's lady time

2. **A good friend you haven't seen in a while comes to town last minute on a Saturday night. He:**

   a Whines that he never gets to spend time with me

   b Says, "I'll make dinner for three, then!"

   c Asks if he can join us for drinks later in the evening

   d Says in that case he'll visit his parents this weekend

   e Asks, "The hot one in the photo by your bed?"

3. Your best friend is tired of hearing:

a About him treating me like shit

b How *great* he is, she gets it

c How *great* he is, she doesn't buy it

d His opinions about things she told me in confidence

e The White Stripes song that was playing when I met him

4. Your best friend is having a dinner party. He:

a Disappointedly asks, "Is anyone *fun* going to be there?"

b Gets mysteriously ill

c Quietly stays by my side, looking distracted

d Says, "What can I bring?"

e Makes so much conversation, I hardly see him all night

5. Circle any of the following your friends might use to describe him:

a Keeper

b Creepy

c Cocky

d Drunky

e Funny

6. You two fight, and you consult your friends about it. He:

   a Says he doesn't want them knowing his business

   b Understands that's what women do

   c Says in that case he's telling his friends I lost his autographed picture of Vin Diesel

   d Hopes that some things are kept between the two of us

   e Makes fun of what they had to say

7. Your guy friends:

   a Introduced him to me

   b Are now his friends, too

   c Make him feel insecure and jealous, no matter what I do

   d Don't like how possessive he acts toward me

   e Always feel intimidated by him

8. How large is his group of friends?

   a He shakes so many hands when we're out, it's like he's the mayor

   b One—me

   c A few people who have known each other a long time

d Depends who's at the OTB

e The Ronman!

9. When he's with all his friends:

a It's all inside jokes; I feel left out

b I like him even more

c I end up playing drinking games 'til the bar closes down

d I'm never there

e I end up talking to their girlfriends all night

10. What best describes the way his friends interact with him?

a Family reunion

b Frat brothers

c Sounds of silence

d Fan club

e WWE

11. He has this one female friend who pays a little too much attention to him:

a He says I'm being paranoid

b He says he'll spend less time with her

c He says, "Well, she is my sister . . ."

d He makes sure when she's around, I'm there, too

e He knows it's true but makes lame excuses for her behavior

12. You tell him one of his friends made a pass at you. He:

a Makes him apologize

b Breaks off the friendship

c Laughs it off

d Doesn't believe me

e Beats him up

13. You can't stand his best friend no matter how hard you try. He:

a Doesn't mind; I'm welcome to my opinion

b Doesn't listen; why should he care?

c Keeps trying

d Stops hanging out with him

e Doesn't get it; "The Ronman is awesome!"

14. Movie that best represents his friends:

a *St. Elmo's Fire*

b *Sixteen Candles*

c *The Breakfast Club*

d *Pretty in Pink*

e *Home Alone*

The Score

1. **a** 4, **b** 4, **c** 2, **d** 1, **e** 3
2. **a** 2, **b** 4, **c** 3, **d** 2, **e** 1
3. **a** 1, **b** 4, **c** 2, **d** 2, **e** 3
4. **a** 1, **b** 2, **c** 2, **d** 4, **e** 3
5. **a** 4, **b** −1, **c** 2, **d** −1, **e** 3
6. **a** 2, **b** 4, **c** 1, **d** 3, **e** 2
7. **a** 4, **b** 3, **c** 2, **d** 1, **e** 2
8. **a** 4, **b** 2, **c** 3, **d** 1, **e** 1
9. **a** 1, **b** 4, **c** 3, **d** 1, **e** 2
10. **a** 4, **b** 2, **c** 1, **d** 3, **e** 1
11. **a** 1, **b** 4, **c** 3, **d** 3, **e** 2
12. **a** 3, **b** 4, **c** 2, **d** 1, **e** 1
13. **a** 4, **b** 2, **c** 3, **d** 1, **e** 1
14. **a** 2, **b** 4, **c** 3, **d** 4, **e** 1

45–56: BFF.

He fits right in and now both of you have increased your circle of friends twofold. Your friends like him. His friends like you. Finally, the relationship that fits in with your relationships.

33–44: Much respect due.

He doesn't dive right in, but he sticks a toe in the water. He understands that your relationships have a place in your life that's important, even if he's not snuggling up on the couch giving your friends dating advice. This is a good workable balance.

22–32: Swept away.

Not a great remake, not a great way to be with your guy. No relationship is an island. It's hard enough to make one a picnic. I don't know what you have to gain by dating a guy without good friendships and without an interest in yours, except eventual loneliness if this doesn't work out. And even if it does.

12–21: Bad blood.

It's a mess, and it's all over everything. Someone's going to be found guilty of something. He clearly is not good at this friends thing. You're clearly not good at this getting along with his friends thing. Boundaries are being crossed, lines are being stepped over, and you're getting trampled underfoot, not to mention swept under the carpet. Plus, he tells you your friends are hot. Yuck.

Chapter 8 score: _____

Cumulative score: _____

Getting the Last Word In

Can your guy be too attentive? Yes. But then we call it clingy. If this should occur, gently and lovingly encourage him to, well, get a life. Maybe you could say it like this: "Um, sweetie, I can wash my own hair." It's great to have someone in your corner, someone who is a support system and takes an active interest in your life, but not to the detriment of his own. Eventually he will cease to be interesting to you and besides, your friends won't want to have him around if it never feels like a choice. Overprotective equals underattractive. It's a thin line between between doting and dull, and he needs to learn to balance on that line like he's in Cirque de So-lady. (Cirque de So-sorry for that pun.)

Signs that your guy may need to get a life:

He surprises (!) your friends by picking up your cell phone when they call you to chat.

He knows your schedule better than you know it.

When people ask what his hobbies are, he says you.

He's on a first-name basis with your hairdresser.

A night out with the guys means watching *The Usual Suspects* at home alone.

When people ask his opinion, he answers using "we" instead of "I."

When your friends all get together, strangely it's always "Ladies' Night."

He responds *for* you: "Hey, you, how was your pre-sentation at work?" Him: "She did great!"

He tells people what you would think of a situation when you're not even there.

He won't buy anything without consulting you first.

He tells your friends how hot you are.

He wears your underwear.

He refers to your dog as "our baby."

The Ex Factor

Some guys remain close with their ex-girlfriends. Much like having a leaky boat on a winding river in a hard rain, this can be a tough one to navigate. More than any other relationship, this one brings up jealousy, suspicion, and insecurity. It can also be a funhouse mirror, and you know what that means. Not so fun. Wow, he dated a woman with a belly ring *and* a tattoo on the small of her back who thinks Dave Matthews "rocks out"? How is it he's also dating you? How can he possibly like two such disparate ladies?

Is it possible for your guy to have a healthy relationship with his ex? Yes, and it may even be a good sign. If someone who went through a breakup with him is still speaking to him, that's a pretty good guy. However, there's also the I-can't-stand-to-think-someone-might-ever-be-unhappy-with-me guy who will maintain these relationships just so no one is ever unhappy with him (hence the name). Very possibly this guy is spreading himself way too thin. If he has a roster of exes he has to socialize with, where will you fit in? And there's also the guy with the jealous ex-girlfriend in the picture, the one who shows up uninvited, who still hangs out with his friends, who says the baby is his. He may paint her as a crazy person, but bear in mind, he's still holding the brush. He can take her out of the picture. *Really?* Is she truly crazy? So much so that no matter what he does, she refuses to go away? Well, then he should program the number of his police precinct into his cell phone. Anything else is a wake-up call to you, and it just might be her calling over and over and over again at four A.M. If he's still involved with Miss Crazy Universe, frankly, he's not available to you. And that is his fault, not hers, no matter what he needs you to think so you won't dump him.

So how do you know what's a healthy relationship with an ex and what's your own jealousy getting in the way? A table, of course.

Healthy	Stealthy
Meeting for dinner	Drinks for two 'til four A.M.
Group outings	Family vacations
Telling you her name	Yelling her name in bed
Lively discussions	Screaming fights
Talking to her from time to time	Talking about her all the time
Having her over	Letting her crash
Introducing her to you	Comparing you to her
A kiss on the cheek	Dancing cheek-to-cheek
Sending presents in the mail	Sending bricks through his window
Picking her up at the airport	Bailing her out of jail

PART THREE

Looking to the Future

You're actually considering forsaking all other guys for This One Guy. Wow . . . are you sure? Lady! The next great guy could be the next guy you meet. Think about all the guys you'll be missing out on dating (and scoring, for that matter. Please, I need to sell this thing). Are you sure he's The One? There are some serious things we need to consider if you're thinking of betting a lifetime on this horse. When this horse breaks a leg, you're going to be the one feeding him and renting him videos . . . because they don't shoot guys, do they?

Time to take a serious look at what's looking really serious. Is his home his castle or your dungeon? Is his job about him following his passion or trying your patience? Is his family a welcome addition or an annoying distraction? And does he score high enough to consider making that ultimate commitment—'til divorce do you part? If you're thinking of going for the gold, you best be sure you've picked a great partner. Sure, he's a hockey player and you're a figure skater, he's hotheaded and you're a perfectionist, these things happen. If you move forward with your eyes wide open, before you even step out on the ice, he'll declare, "I'm saying I love you. I'm saying it out loud!" and you'll glide through the program seemlessly, executing the most difficult move of all—the Fremchenko! (That's our metaphor for marriage. I know it's a stretch.) But you know what happens when you skate blind. No matter how well-intentioned all concerned parties are—you forget about the flowers. You snag a skate. You fall flat on your ass. So let's score a few final things. After all, your skirt is short and that ice is hard. And cold.

The Gay Boyfriend: The Must-Have Accessory

Let's get it straight, as it were. You have a Gay Boyfriend, and your secondary boyfriend is going to have to get used to it. He must put aside any and all lingering homophobia and embrace it, even embrace him, from here on out—possibly have his ass squeezed from time to time. But only if he has a really good ass. If you are going to be really serious with this guy, he must entertain the idea of your Gay Boyfriend, while your Gay Boyfriend entertains you by voguing around your living room, singing, "She's your dream girl—dream girls will make you happy!" Did I mention he's doing it in a wig? Well, he is. And that straight guy who's always hanging around, ruining all your fun by asking questions like, "Who's Julie Newmar?" or "Who's Lucky Pierre?" or referring to David LaChapelle as Dave Chappelle or misquoting lines from *Mommie Dearest* just has to accept into his life, his heart, and his brunches the man you were truly meant to be with. Because in truth you are a gay man, trapped in a drag queen, trapped in a woman's body. Girl.

Your Gay Boyfriend is the person who admires all the things about you your straight one is supposed to: new dress, great shoes, highlights in your hair, cute earrings, half a pound lost, hilarious joke about Christina Aguilera, songs from musicals sung out loud in restaurants, jazz hands, Ketel One. (How can he not admire the things that sustain his people?) Who will appreciate all this if you don't have your Gay Boyfriend? Who will say things like "Gurrrl, you look *fabulous!*" or "That is a *fabulous* bag, Miss One!" or "*Fabulous!*" Who will say those myriad things if he isn't there?

Your Gay Boyfriend is like the sand to your straight boyfriend's jar of marbles. He fills in all the empty spaces. He'll not only tell you which pair of shoes he likes best, he'll tell you why. He'll tell you another woman doesn't look as fierce as you, even if she really is truly very fierce. He can cook. You can eat. You look better when you're on his arm because there's room on his arm for you, a martini, a cigarette, a BlackBerry, and a piece of cake. With your Gay Boyfriend life's a piece of cake—a great big chocolately pink-and-yellow-frosted piece of cake with a rose on it. You can't go it without him, nor should you.

Other boyfriends take heed. He's here. He's queer. Get used to him. What is your guy so freaked out about, anyway? It's not like you're cheating on him. This other man likes other men.

CHAPTER 9

THINKING INSIDE THE BOX

 His Apartment

Have you ever been lucky enough to date that one rare guy who cares about what his apartment looks like? Who hand picked his desk from a really cool local furniture company? Who painted his dresser himself with how-to kung fu instructions? Who doesn't have a CD tower? Maybe his bed actually has a blanket and a full set of sheets. That match each other. Drum roll . . . that even match the pillow cases. He has a spice rack. He has some art on the walls. His bath mat isn't just a crumpled, slightly damp towel. None of the furniture in his apartment was made by him in junior high woodworking class. And when you sit on his toilet, you don't feel like you're going to catch something. Never leave, my lady, never leave. Just like Toyland, your youth, and the VIP section at Studio 54, once you pass its borders you can never go back again.

Let's don our hazmat suits and walk into every other guy's apartment, shall we? A guy's apartment is calculus. It's a problem we have no way of solving. It's a problem whose very existence puzzles us in the first place. What practical application can the apartment have? Why would sheets be made of polyester? . . . *No answer.* What is the benefit of using Saran wrap over the windows in the winter? . . . *Sorry, I'm drawing a blank.* Shouldn't the toothbrush be in the toothbrush holder, rather than wrapped in aluminum foil? . . . *I'll take a pass on that one.* Does he really like the Mariah Carey movie *Glitter*—why else would a framed poster for it be hanging on his wall? How is it possible for dust to collect in the toilet-paper holder? It's as if guys are on a reality show and have been challenged to survive with only seven coat hangers, a few tiny take-out creamers from the deli, an eleven-year-old desk lamp, and a really good computer. And yet they call these places home. With their bed frames held up by three legs and one pile of paperback books. With litter boxes in their bedrooms. With packets of "cock soup mix" taped to their walls for décor. Like animals, they seem not to care about comfort or window treatments. Their cave is simply a place to find shelter for the night, share the spoils of the hunt (buffalo wings), and get dressed for another day of survival in the wild.

And then there's apartment etiquette, which may be nonexistent in his place and only slightly more in evidence at yours. When you visit his apartment do you marvel at the famous Leaning Tower of Pizza Take-Out Boxes? What's with the pile of balled-up used Kleenex just sitting mid–coffee table? When you ask if he has an extra toothbrush you can use, does he answer, "Just use the one I use—my roommate's." I hate to bring up a tired old cliché, but really, they can put a man on the moon, but if there's a toilet there when he arrives, he won't put the seat down.

The Quiz: The House That Jack or Tim or Dan Built

1. On his walls:

  a Confederate flag

  b Framed art that he picked out

  c A "sexy" silhouette of a naked woman

  d *Star Wars* poster(s)

2. His couch:

  a Black leather

  b Super-comfy

  c Belongs in the street where it came from

  d Futon!

3. The screen saver on his computer is:

a The St. Pauli Girl

b A scantily clad Pam Anderson

c The Botticelli Venus

d Tommy Lee playing with Mötley Crüe

4. What do you find when you use the bathroom?

a Toilet paper

b A sock

c Paper towel

d Yesterday's news

5. His shower:

a Is that soap or lava rock?

b I'm not sure if the water's coming from the showerhead or the hole in the ceiling

c Has a curtain *and* a liner

d Is a scientific lab, dedicated to growing mold

6. You know when he last cleaned the tub by:

a Counting the rings

b Counting on the cleaning lady

c Counting back to the day he moved in

d Counting the number of times he complains his back hurts

7. Circle any item found in his medicine cabinet or thereabouts:

Preparation H

Icy Hot

Dandruff shampoo

Propecia

Conditioner

Home waxing kit

Hair gel

Hair spray

Crack Creme

Old Spice

Your friend Christina's
phone number on a slip
of crumpled-up paper

Mouthwash

Valtrex

Face lotion

Body lotion

K-Y Jelly

Nail clippers

Tampons/pads

Viagra

Lip balm

8. Where can you throw out garbage?

a The garbage can

b Plastic bags hung around the kitchen

c The pile in the corner with the incense burning next to it

d Anywhere there's still floor showing

9. What's in his sink?

a A never-ending pile of dirty dishes

b Chrome alone

c Water that won't drain for a couple of days

d A shirt his roommate's tie-dyeing

10. He uses his oven for:

a Storing his comic-book collection

b Baking pies

c Heating up frozen dinners for us

d Reheating food his mom sends over in marked Tupperware

11. In his cupboards you find:

a Sigma Chi "Party 'Til You Die" beer mug

b A can of coffee and one coffee cup

c A set of matching dishes for eight people

d Roaches

12. Inside his fridge:

a Soy sauce packets, ketchup packets, and a half-empty two-liter bottle of Diet Coke

b Beer and batteries

c UTO—unidentifiable take-out

d Dust

1 3. You open up his freezer when you need:

a Ice that tastes like plastic

b Two-year-old frozen burritos

c Freezer burn

d A good bottle of vodka

1 4. You eat dinner at:

a The kitchen table

b The coffee table in front of the TV

c The dining-room table

d The cardboard box turned upside down with a dish towel over it

1 5. A table setting consists of:

a Chopsticks for hamburgers?

b Plate, fork, knife, spoon, napkin, glass

c Plastic utensils and napkin packet left over from delivery

d Knees and paper towel

1 6. It's too darn hot:

a He turns on the air conditioner

b He turns on the fan

c He makes you a paper fan

d He sweats buckets

17. In the bedroom?

   a A lawn chair

   b Neat bed, bed table, bureau

   c Ten years of *Popular Mechanics* subscriptions

   d Everything!!! (sound of plate smashing)

18. In a word, his bed is:

   a Heavenly

   b Hellish

   c Twin

   d Futon!

19. His sheets are:

   a Hunt Club

   b Sheets, plural? He only has one set.

   c Five-hundred-thread-count Egyptian cotton

   d *Battlestar Galactica*

20. The weirdest thing in his bedroom

   a The StairMaster

   b The Carmen Electra doll

   c The video camera

   d The roll of hundred-dollar bills hidden in the sock drawer

The Score

1. a 1, b 4, c 3, d 2
2. a 3, b 4, c 1, d 2
3. a 2, b 3, c 4, d 1
4. a 4, b 2, c 3, d 1
5. a 3, b 1, c 4, d 2
6. a 3, b 4, c 1, d 2
7. See table
8. a 4, b 3, c 2, d 1
9. a 3, b 4, c 1, d 2
10. a 1, b 4, c 3, d 2
11. a 2, b 3, c 4, d 1
12. a 3, b 2, c 4, d 1
13. a 3, b 2, c 1, d 4
14. a 3, b 2, c 4, d 1
15. a 2, b 4, c 3, d 1
16. a 4, b 3, c 2, d 1
17. a 3, b 4, c 2, d 1
18. a 4, b 3, c 1, d 2
19. a 3, b 1, c 4, d 2
20. a 4, b 3, c 2, d 1

Question 7 Table

−1	+2
Preparation H	Conditioner
Dandruff shampoo	Icy Hot
Propecia	Mouthwash
Home waxing kit	Face lotion
Hair spray	Hair gel
Crack Creme	Body lotion
Old Spice	Nail clippers
Your friend Christina's phone number on a slip of crumpled-up paper	Tampons/pads
	Lip balm
Valtrex	K-Y Jelly
Viagra	

75–96: Housekeeper.

Hooray, this guy has a handle on his domicile. It's all happening— an empty sink, utensils, a bed with sheets. How can you stand this embarrassment of riches? How can you live with yourself, having so much when others go without? I don't mean to criticize, but I'm not sure how you can sleep at night on that 500-thread-count Egyptian cotton.

53–74: Average slob.

It's not great, but it's bearable. He may not have exquisite taste, but he cleans up once in a while, and you can actually see the floor. And at least he has some coffee in the cupboard for the morning.

31–52: Straight out of college.

I hope he graduated just last year because he lives like he did. He's going to have to grow up, move away from the makeshift, the giveaways, the hand-me-downs, the *Star Wars* posters (unless he's George Lucas!).

9–30: Garbage collector.

Don't touch anything!!! Now get out of there and shower. Tomorrow it will all be a bad memory.

> ***Question Exception:** If you answered "futon" twice, once for his couch and once for his bed, well, you need to subtract 5 points from his score. Fold it up for the last time.

Chapter 9 score: _____

Cumulative score: _____

Getting the Last Word In

The day may never come when your guy offhandedly says, "I was thinking a couple of throw rugs might add some color to this room. Let's go look at some tomorrow." But in this case, that may be good news. When you move in with your guy, do you really want to have to take his opinion into account? (Hint: Unless you want Three Stooges commemorative wallpaper—no.) It calls to mind the story of a friend who was dismayed to find that when she moved in with her boyfriend, she also had to cohabitate with the colonial-style bureau he'd had since childhood, complete with its original 1976 bicentennial contact paper lining the drawers. When she tried to convince him it was hideous and he should get rid of it, rather than appealing to her emotions by explaining that it had sentimental value, he insisted that it was *really nice*. No argument she made could convince him that her pursuit of happiness was being compromised by the piece of furniture that held his socks. His bureau went with him to his next apartment, but she did not.

Imagine what else might be considered *really nice*—a massage chair, his collection of plastic mugs from his cross-country trip, a macaroni sculpture of his dog he made when he was seven. Go on. Let him eat off old TV trays his parents brought from home the last time they visited. Those are easy to leave on the street when you guys finally shack up together. And in the meantime, hang out at your place.

CHAPTER 10

WORK TO DO

Job

Lots of people believe that what you do isn't who you are. And those people sell babies on the black market. When someone says, "I'm a doctor," your heart still flutters inexplicably. Thank God, then, that there's a doctor in the house. Hello! When a guy tells you he's in a band that you've never heard of, you're still totally impressed (twenties), slightly suspicious (thirties), or completely exhausted (forties). You care what your guy does. When someone asks, "What does your guy do for a living?" you want to be able to say something really cool, like he's a researcher at the robot lab at MIT or he's working on zero-calorie chocolate. Let the aristrocrats with family money who never had to work for a living in the first place be offended by the question of what someone does to earn one. Let them scoff at our uncouth ways. The rest of us don't have that luxury. For us, the sad reality is that we get up five out of every seven days a week at some ungodly hour, like before noon, and have to wash our faces, brush our teeth, and put on clothes just to piss away hours and hours that we'll never get back, cooped up with people who just happened to end up in the same place we did. Most of us strive to soften this blow as much as possible by eventually finding something that gives us satisfaction or at the very least, keeps our neck out of the noose. It's important to you. It should be important to him. No matter what stance you take at the start, over time, without proper care, complications will occur.

I've heard women bravely claim they don't care what their guy does, as long as he's a good person. I admire the sentiment. It's really, really, really wonderful (*three* reallys). It's also never going to work. And he may work slightly less than that. I know you, lady. You are not going to be happy in ten years with a bike messenger who gets high every day, no matter how well he treats you. You don't really want to tell your friends that the love of your life is a barista at Starbucks while waiting to . . . do nothing else. Accountant? Throw my key in the fishbowl; maybe I'll get lucky tonight! Let's break it down into completely overgeneralized categories. Come on, it'll be fun!

Money for Money's Sake Guy:

This guy is the most dangerous: The lawyer you're dating today is the stand-up comic who's on the road three-quarters of the year tomorrow. This is the guy who's going to provide you with all the amenities you think you want—the amazing vacations, the new car with the giant bow on top (how do they get those bows on those cars?), the delicious steaks cooked to buttery perfection—but he's also the guy who may inexplicably decide to move to Maine and become a lobsterman. If your guy is doing something he doesn't care about seven, eight, twenty-five hours a day, just to make a buck, he's probably not coming home feeling satisfied. Even if he's making a lot of bucks, he may still feel unfulfilled. Hey, there's a chance that all he wants to do is slave his entire life away so you can have nice things. But there's also a chance that he'll want to explore modern dance or Tahiti or another relationship.

Never Give Up the Dream Guy:

This guy has passion to spare, but probably not cash. Yes, we love this guy. We applaud him for making the short film, writing the Great American Novel, singing with the nondenominational choir. But one day you're gonna wake up and realize a well-arranged choral version of Lionel Richie's "Hello" isn't going to put a down payment on a house. The guitar solo from "Stairway to Heaven" isn't going to pay for groceries. A poetry slam can't fix a broken window. Maybe not even a broken heart. He's living the dream while you're dreaming of a nice meal once in a while. Go on and love him, lady, but know what you're in for. In for a penny, in for tens of thousands of dollars of your own hard-earned cash. He may know the lyrics to every song written by Bread, but you may end up being the breadwinner.

On the Verge Guy:

How is he? He's *great!!* Every week this guy is almost about to "make it." There is something amazing just about to happen that's going to change everything that he can't really quite tell you about, even though he's always telling you about it and then . . . it never happens. Take us off your e-mail list, for Christ's sake!

Super Success:

The name says it all. These are the guys who found something they love to do and through a combination of dogged determination, unwavering self-confidence, tunnel vision, and good luck have managed to succeed at it. They've worked for many years to build something they can be proud of—a business, a performing career, a chain of restaurants. They're accomplished, full of energy, gregarious. Everybody wants to be around them. They've worked so hard that their relationships may have been a second thought. Then they finally slow down and take a look around and realize they're forty and they're alone. So they date nineteen-year-olds.

The Quiz: Work It, Boy

Due to some totally crazy circumstances, like getting fired for stealing hanging file folders, your guy loses his job. Due to some crazier circumstances, like being scored by you, he is offered the jobs in each group below and has to take one. Which one is he most suited for? Rate them from 1, best fit, to 4, worst fit.

1. ___ **a** Stand-up comic

   ___ **b** Clown

   ___ **c** Comedy writer

   ___ **d** Syndicated cartoonist

2. ___ **a** Cowboy

   ___ **b** Urban Cowboy

   ___ **c** Midnight Cowboy

   ___ **d** Dancer in Agnes de Mille's (*Rodeo*)

3. ___ **a** Film director

   ___ **b** Producer

   ___ **c** Best boy

   ___ **d** Craft services

4. ___ **a** Jazz singer

   ___ **b** Rabbi

   ___ **c** Cantor

   ___ **d** Mohel

5. ___ **a** Resaurant owner

___ **b** Busboy

___ **c** Waiter

___ **d** Chef

6. ___ **a** Tinker

___ **b** Tailor

___ **c** Soldier

___ **d** Spy

7. ___ **a** TV star

___ **b** Movie star

___ **c** Theater star

___ **d** Superstar

8. ___ **a** Counter at McDonald's

___ **b** Counter at Taco Bell

___ **c** Counter at KFC

___ **d** Counter at Donut Pub

9. ___ **a** Baseball player

___ **b** Basketballer

___ **c** Golfer

___ **d** Tennis pro

10. ___ **a** Backup dancer for Britney

___ **b** Backup dancer for Christina

___ **c** Backup dancer for Liza

___ **d** Thunder from Down Under dancer

11. ___ **a** Video game programmer

___ **b** IT consultant

___ **c** Webmaster for Spockwatch.com

___ **d** Creator of Google

12. ___ **a** DJ at a strip club

___ **b** First-chair violinist, New York Philharmonic

___ **b** Church organist

___ **c** The Piano Man

13. ___ **a** Subway planner

___ **b** Subway conductor

___ **c** Subway cop

___ **d** Jared

14. ___ **a** Poet

___ **b** Modern dancer

___ **c** Theremin player

___ **d** Wig maker

15. ___ **a** Gambler

    ___ **b** Stockbroker

    ___ **c** Realtor

    ___ **d** Insurance salesman

16. ___ **a** Lawyer

    ___ **b** Publicist

    ___ **c** Politician

    ___ **d** Stable boy

17. ___ **a** Teller

    ___ **b** Prison guard

    ___ **c** Lion tamer

    ___ **d** Jockey

18. ___ **a** Heavy metal god

    ___ **b** Hip-hop hustler

    ___ **c** Country boy

    ___ **d** Lithuanian folk dancer

19. ___ **a** Hockey player

    ___ **b** Boxer

    ___ **c** Stuntman

    ___ **d** Dentist

20. ___ **a** Surgeon

___ **b** Fireman

___ **c** Lifeguard

___ **d** Evangelical preacher

The Score

I've rated the job choices in terms of coolness—1, most cool, 4, least cool. Surprise! When you match all four of my ratings—3 points. Match 2—2 points. Match 1—1 point. Match none—you guessed it—0.

1. a 2   **2. a** 1   **3. a** 1

  b 4   **b** 3   **b** 3

  c 1   **c** 4   **c** 4

  d 3   **d** 2   **d** 2

4. a 1   **5. a** 2   **6. a** 3

  b 3   **b** 4   **b** 2

  c 2   **c** 3   **c** 4

  d 4   **d** 1   **d** 1

7. a 4   **8. a** 3   **9. a** 3

  b 2   **b** 2   **b** 1

  c 3   **c** 4   **c** 4

  d 1   **d** 1   **d** 2

10. **a** 3
    b 2
    c 1
    d 4

11. **a** 2
    b 3
    c 4
    d 1

12. **a** 4
    b 1
    c 3
    d 2

13. **a** 1
    b 3
    c 2
    d 4

14. **a** 3
    b 1
    c 2
    d 4

15. **a** 1
    b 3
    c 2
    d 4

16. **a** 2
    b 4
    c 3
    d 1

17. **a** 3
    b 4
    c 1
    d 2

18. **a** 2
    b 1
    c 3
    d 4

19. **a** 2
    b 3
    c 1
    d 4

20. **a** 1
    b 2
    c 3
    d 4

41–60: CEO.
Your guy is suited for a cool job. Which makes him hot.

2 1–40: Middle management.

No need to be embarrassed. You can tell your parents what he does. You can even tell your judgmental friends. You may not be invited to every VIP party, but they get so tedious after a while.

0–20: You're fired!

The Thunder from Down Under? Really?

---

*Question exception: If your guy actually has one of the jobs mentioned in this section, add 5 points!

Chapter 1 0 score: _____

Cumulative score: _____

Getting the Last Word In

Don't shit where you eat. You've heard it a million times, although you might not have understood it the first couple. Why would anyone go to the bathroom in the kitchen? Gross. (Maybe I still don't understand it.) But even the sage advice of someone possibly locked in a bathroom with lunch in hand can't keep us from the taboo of getting busy in the place where we should be keeping busy—the workplace. Sounds exciting, doesn't it? Gives a whole new meaning to one lawyer asking another to see his briefs. A whole new meaning to one carpenter imploring another to give him a screw. A whole new meaning to one chef asking another to cover him in whipped cream and lick it off. (Sorry, that last one has the same meaning it always had.)

The problem with workplace romance is the workplace part. You no longer take the elevator; now you take the Hellevator. You press the button and wait, sweating, hoping to avoid being trapped in a cramped space with the person you were sweaty and naked with in a cramped space only one short week ago. And on those days when you must ride together, you must use every ounce of your will not to yell to unsuspecting coworkers, "He can't get it up, and he dumped *me!*" One wrong move at the holiday party after-party that's not officially sanctioned by your company, and now you're doomed to skittering down the halls, hoping you don't have to work with Creative Services anytime soon.

There's only one foolproof way to have a workplace romance. It comes but once a year, it has but one word in its title: intern. You heard me. Who else can you be sure you'll be superior to, so you won't have to deal with suing him for sexual harassment when he doesn't promote you after you've clocked in hours of overtime? The intern is going to leave anyway. He won't be in the halls or the Hellevator in the fall. And news flash: He's hot! I don't mean slightly graying, only one divorce, at least he has a weekend house normal workplace guy hot. I mean track team, Dickens in his messenger bag, he hasn't given up on life hot. He's smokin' hot! Get him to change your toner! (Honestly, no idea what that means.) He's there to learn. You're there to learn new ways to get through another day. He's there to spend his family's money. You're there to show him where to go to dinner. He's there to work his way into a full-time job. You're there to make sure his résumé gets lost on its way to HR. This thing could really benefit both of you. So what are you waiting for? Get to work.

CHAPTER 11

TOO CLOSE FOR COMFORT

Family

It was Andy Gibb (RIP) who sang, "Love is higher than a mountain/ Love is thicker than water." Some would disagree and say blood is thicker than water, but honestly a few stiff drinks should take care of that problem. When it comes right down to the wire, love should triumph over blood. Simply put, it's freaky when a guy is way too close to his family. And by his family, of course I mean his mother. Guys can have all kinds of issues with their fathers, issues that can take years of therapy, antidepressants, and martial-arts training to get through. The overbearing father who made him feel like he was never good enough. The absent father who didn't love him enough. The gay father who remains closeted to this day. The gay father who came out later in life and promptly brought Gary home for the holidays. But those problems are a drop in bucket compared to Hurricane Margie or Olive or Bitsy.

Men and their mothers. These are the Alcatraz of relationships. Built to be inescapable, those who have tried to do so have been severely punished. And even when finally released for good behavior, they remain haunted by their time there. Many serve life sentences. The story that follows is about one such unlucky man and one even unluckier lady. A friend once dated an actor who she accompanied on a job because as luck would have it, it was in an exotic location. When his work was done, they found themselves alone together on a private beach, embracing under a tropical moon. It was so gorgeous and so romantic, surely nothing could sully the moment they were sharing. He kissed her, and then turned to her just like in the movies and said, "You know what's so great about that moon? Right now it's shining on my mother, too." They say it's hard to run in sand. Try running away in it. Apparently, this catch also had a photo of his mom on his bedside table. Nothing like his mom having the best seat in the house for the live show. Hey, Manchurian Candidate, time for a little deprogramming, don'tcha think?

Then there's the guy whose tumultuous relationship

with his mom colors all his relationships with and feelings about other women. You remind him of his mom too much, you don't remind him of his mom enough, he needs to take care of his mom, he can't get far enough away from her, he secretly despises all women because his mom was a relentless critic, he can't love enough women to prove he's lovable to his mom—it just goes on and on, not unlike this sentence. His mom is always there, hovering above him like Tinker Bell (who also had her abandonment issues, if you'll recall), whispering in his ear and demanding his attention, always ready to find fault with you. Thank God you've never been asked to clap her back to life because you might experience an unexpected loss of motor skills and rhythm. But maybe this guy, who longs to break these chains of love, is better than the guy who was so spoiled by his mom that he doesn't know he has a finger to lift. If your guy expects you to not only cook, clean, and launder for him, but to do it in a particular way to which he's become accustomed, chances are another woman has been more than willing to do it for him for years. How can you compete? Better question—would you ever want to?

The Quiz: It's a Family Affair

1. Which TV show most reminds you of his family?

a *Arrested Development*

b *7th Heaven*

c *Eight Is Enough*

2. The first time you have dinner with his parents:

   a It's so quiet, I can hear myself swallow

   b There's lively conversation about the news, the arts, your lives

   c His dad flirts with me. He warned me—his dad's crazy!

3. Which word would he use to describe his mother?

   a Maid

   b Mentor

   c Queen

4. His mother tells him she's offended by "something you did":

   a He talks to her privately, calming her down

   b Houston, we have a problem, and it's me!

   c He tells her to get out. Now

5. When his mother calls, it's usually to:

   a Remind him to take a jacket to work; it's getting cold!

   b Borrow money

   c Catch up on everyone's lives and illnesses

6. When his father calls, it's usually to:

a Give him shit about getting a better job

b Talk baseball scores

c Remind him to call his mother, she misses him!

7. His family wants you to come visit:

a We agree to spend *three* days—and bring some good wine

b He yells at me to never take his sister's phone calls again—she's dead to him!

c We walk upstairs. What? He's Italian

8. He tells his mom you're a vegetarian. For dinner you get served:

a What everyone else is eating; there's veggie stuff on the menu

b A big, juicy rare steak

c Eighteen deviled eggs on a plate. Yum

9. When he gets together with his siblings it's all:

a Seven straight hours of home movies

b Family jokes around the dining-room table

c Move, you're blocking the TV!

10. **His "high maintenance" brother wants to rent a room from you. He:**

   a Changes all the locks and gets a guard dog

   b Thinks it would be a good way for him to learn responsibility on the outside

   c Lets him down easy

11. **His mom always wished he would get:**

   a A nose job

   b Ahead on his own terms

   c A house down the street

12. **When he calls his mom, it's to:**

   a Laugh with her

   b Cry to her

   c Yell at her

13. **What makes you feel like part of his family?**

   a Seven drinks

   b Getting to know them over time

   c Prayer circle

14. He's accompanying you to your parents' house:

a He brings a thoughtful gift for them

b He tells the story of losing his virginity at the dinner table

c He watches the *America's Next Top Model* marathon

15. On his family vacation you go to:

a Their timeshare at Disneyland on Pleasure Island

b Their summer home on Fire Island

c Riker's Island for visiting hours

16. It's family game time!

a Truth or Dare

b Trivial Pursuit

c Candy Land

17. His mother can't wait for you to have a baby!

a He asks why his brother's brats aren't enough for her

b He says he'll talk to me about it

c He explains to her that I might want to be involved in that decision

18. **You finally find the time to take that vacation you've been planning on!**

   a Miami's out because of his father's restraining order against him

   b His seven cousins end up sleeping on our floor and going everywhere with us

   c A family vacation is out

19. **Which of the following might you overhear at his family reunion (for the sake of this question, your guy is temporarily named Pete):**

   a She's not as cool as Pete's first wife!

   b God love her, she fits right in

   c No matter what, Pete will always be my little boy

   a Oops, I better go save her from Uncle Harry

   b Looks like someone put on a little weight . . .

   c Isn't Peter gorgeous? I tell you, if I hadn't married his father, I'd be dating him!

   a She may be his girlfriend, but I'm still his prettiest cousin

   b Don't worry, she eats anything

   c I think Peter is in love at last!

The Score

1. **a** 3, **b** 2, **c** 1
2. **a** 1, **b** 3, **c** 2
3. **a** 1, **b** 3, **c** 2
4. **a** 3, **b** 2, **c** 1
5. **a** 2, **b** 1, **c** 3
6. **a** 1, **b** 3, **c** 2
7. **a** 3, **b** 1, **c** 2
8. **a** 3, **b** 1, **c** 2
9. **a** 2, **b** 3, **c** 1
10. **a** 1, **b** 2, **c** 3
11. **a** 1, **b** 3, **c** 2
12. **a** 3, **b** 2, **c** 1
13. **a** 1, **b** 3, **c** 2
14. **a** 3, **b** 2, **c** 1
15. **a** 2, **b** 3, **c** 1
16. **a** 1, **b** 3, **c** 2
17. **a** 1, **b** 2, **c** 3
18. **a** 1, **b** 2, **c** 3
19. **a** 1, **b** 3, **c** 2
    a 3, **b** 1, **c** 2
    a 2, **b** 1, **c** 3

49–63: They are fa-mi-ly.

He loves them, but he still leaves them. And in this case, that's laudable. He takes a healthy distance, but he also has a good relationship with them. He's also willing to address problems with them or tell them when something is none of their business. And they welcome you in. As well they should. 'Cause you're awesome.

35–48: The von Trapps.

Is there a singing competition in Salzburg in their past, maybe a walk across the Alps? Why so close? It's too much, it's too weird, it's going to get in the way. If he's living with his family, that's bad enough. But if he's tied up in their lives and under their spell and he doesn't live with them, that's almost worse. You may have to ease him away. With a crowbar.

21–34: Capturing the Friedmans.

What is going on here? There's so much dysfunction, the von Bulows are shaking their heads. It doesn't bode well for your future when there's this much trouble in his past. Is he in therapy, trying to work through this stuff? I sure as shit hope so. But if not, run. Just run. Those who don't understand their guy's family history are doomed to repeat it—themselves.

> **Chapter 11 score:** _____

> **Cumulative score:** _____

Getting the Last Word in

At the end of the day, after all the therapy, we still want to date someone we can bring home to our families. When you consider dating the rich kid from the other side of town in the '80s movie or the male stripper, you get a little anxious. How will you convince your down-on-his-luck dad who just got laid off from the steel mill that Rake really loves you? Is he going to make you quit Steel Emotion, the band you and Rake formed together? Then who will play at prom? Will the male stripper be able to remember and recite the elaborate fake life you've created for him when he thinks a physicist is the guy who spots you when you're lifting really heavy weights at the gym?

Sure, we worry what our families are going to think about our significant others, but remember—they don't have to date them. You are the one who ultimately has to live with the decision of whether he's right for you. You are the one who knows what he's like beyond his answering twenty bizarre questions designed to determine whether pastry chef is a "real job." At the end of the family visit, you return to your "real life" with him. So he doesn't have a job at the moment, so he never went to college, so he's from a different religious background. So step back, take a deep breath, and remember your parents are almost definitely overprotective and your siblings get a sick pleasure out of making you suffer. And unless you've witnessed him doing something wildly inappropriate in front of your family, like actually telling them he's unemployed—I mean, come on, you have to be a little smart—make your own decisions. And then admit to yourself that the time you brought home that guy with the multiple facial piercings, you were trying to push their buttons.

CHAPTER 12

IS THAT YOUR
FINAL ANSWER?

 *Marriage & Kids*

Look, far be it from me to ever suggest you should get married and have kids. Where's the fun in that? It's not the 1950s anymore, we don't have to be married to have socially acceptable sex, and the species is not exactly at risk. Everything else is at risk, like our natural resources and affordable housing, but the species seems to just keep on booming. We have jobs now, we vote, we wear pants. We have pets. Isn't that enough? For some of you, it's not. Like the Native Americans believed in using every part of the buffalo, you don't believe in letting any part of the man go to waste. You can't get enough of him and must share a dwelling with him and spend all your spare time with him and promise to do it *forever*. You feel the need to harvest part of the man and make another person, somewhat like the man. OK . . . if you really think that's a good idea. Wouldn't you rather just get a massage and rent *The Last Seduction*? Just a thought!

What makes a man marriage material? Do you just *know*? Is it like lightning striking without possible loss of memory? Almost. The difference in the case of marriage is, after your burned hair grows back a few months later, you have potentially fifty-some-odd years to compromise your way through. And unlike celebrities, you're not doing this to promote a new film or because you starred with someone in a new film or in hopes of finally, please God, getting a new film. The Scientologists haven't scientologistically matched you up with a guy by multiplying Maximum Career Enhancement with Beard Factor. You really believe in the shoddily-tended-to "institution" of marriage. You really believe there is one guy for you and that you should make the commitment to show him Endless Love, Always and Forever, Oh, Sherry (if your name happens to be Sherry). Then what you're looking for is that one elusive guy who isn't as fucked up as all the previous guys. The No-Bullshit Guy. This is the guy who you feel most yourself around, who believes in communication and honestly talking through problems. The one who doesn't freak out when he sees you crying in front of the TV, but just walks into the kitchen to get you a pint of ice cream. This is the responsible guy you can depend on.

And then there are those pesky kids. Oh, those rapscallions never give you a moment's peace. They want changing and feeding and caring for. Then they want an education, dance lessons, and allowances. Then it's diplomas, apartments, and inheritances. So needy. Unless you have so much money that you can have them and then have someone else raise them, they are going to change your life forever. And hopefully his life, too. No absent daddy for your kids! This guy is going to be right there, from the delivery room, to kids of their own. But now we're getting ahead of ourselves. Let's just see if he's the type who might change diapers, get up in the middle of the night, and stay home with you and the kid(s) when his friends are out carousing. That is, if he even wants kids. He does want kids, doesn't he?

The Quiz: First Comes Love, Then Comes Marriage...

1. **You attend a wedding together and you catch the bouquet! He:**

   a Applauds wildly and kisses me

   b Says, "Watch it! It almost hit me!"

   c Looks around, laughing nervously

2. You tell him your best friend's husband cheated on her. His response:

   a "That dude was bad news. He has no sense of humor"

   b "All men cheat, baby. That's the way we're wired"

   c "I can't believe it! Chris and Chris were such a great couple! Is Chris OK?"

3. You get a chihuahua. He:

   a Is always aggressively swatting it away

   b Walks it for me when I'm busy

   c Gets right down to its level, rolling around with it and cracking up

4. You ask him where he sees the relationship going:

   a He suggests Cape Cod for a week or so in the summer

   b He opens a beer and laughs nervously

   c He says he can't imagine his life without me

5. You wish he could express his feelings more openly:

   a He agrees maybe it's time for some therapy

   b "OK, this conversation makes me feel nauseous"

   c He laughingly says he'll try . . . every single time we have the conversation

6. You want to baby-sit your two nieces:

a He laughs and says, "For real?"

b He says, "Great! I'll make brownies!"

c He says, "Two? Don't they know about birth control?"

7. You ask him if he wants kids:

a Yes!

b No!

c Ha ha ha ha heee ha ha hee

8. His ideas for kids' names:

a He likes the idea of using family names

b For a boy: Gandalf; for a girl: Xena! Hilarious!

c "Maybe we'll have twins—how about Ball and Chain?"

9. The relationship is at a standstill. You want to take a break:

a He wants to work out our problems together

b "Hey, if you want to take a break, I am out of here"

c Tears of a clown

10. How would he finish this sentence? Marriage is good for:

   a Our future

   b Killing the fun

   c A green card

11. You have to give a speech at a friend's rehearsal dinner and you're super nervous:

   a He makes me laugh so I won't be so freaked out

   b He comes with me to support me

   c "What are you being so dramatic for? It's not like you sing with a band like your friend Christina"

12. You're in the hospital:

   a He visits, looks sicker than I do, and laughs uneasily as he backs out of the room

   b He visits as often as he possibly can, bringing magazines and spending time talking

   c He visits once and tries to pick up a nurse

13. You call him, panicked. There's a giant flying cockroach in your apartment!!

a He tells me to remain calm, isolate myself from the roach—he'll be right over to kill it

b He kills it, and then teases me for being so girly

c "What's your problem?" He lives across town. "Just kill it."

14. Your home is burglarized:

a He stays home, watching *Cops*

b He comforts me, then asks if they took his Richard Pryor albums

c He immediately comes over to see if I'm OK and helps me talk to the police

15. An older woman is struggling with a heavy shopping cart up some stairs. He:

a Jumps to it, helping her

b Doesn't notice

c Smiles at her sympathetically as he passes her on the stairs

16. His big dark secret:

   a He loves the movie *Beaches*

   b He declared bankruptcy a year ago

   c He's a member of the Jeff Foxworthy fan club

17. Which of the following three things would really make him happy?

   a Winning Lotto

   b Great relationship, happy family, fulfilling job

   c The Red Sox winning the World Series again. There's nothing funny about that

The Score

1. a 3, b 1, c 2

2. a 2, b 1, c 3

3. a 1, b 3, c 2

4. a 1, b 2, c 3

5. a 3, b 1, c 2

6. a 2, b 3, c 1

7. a 3, b 1, c 2

8. a 3, b 2, c 1

9. a 3, b 1, c 2

10. a 3, b 2, c 1

11.	**a** 2,	**b** 3,	**c** 1
12.	**a** 2,	**b** 3,	**c** 1
13.	**a** 3,	**b** 2,	**c** 1
14.	**a** 1,	**b** 2,	**c** 3
15.	**a** 3,	**b** 1,	**c** 2
16.	**a** 3,	**b** 1,	**c** 2
17.	**a** 1,	**b** 3,	**c** 2

40–51: Good to go.

This guy wants to move forward. He's comfortable talking about marriage and kids, he's nice to old people, he likes to baby-sit. When the chips are down, he brings the dip. He does nice things for you not because he wants something in return, but because he loves you. Everybody: *Aaaaaaah*. Single tear.

28–39: As you were.

This guy just wants the status quo. He's comfortable in the relationship as is. He doesn't have to think about the future because you do that for him, don't you? So when he's pushed into a corner, his favorite tactic is avoiding the conversation altogether. That's what all the laughter is for. This guy might be a super guy. He's interested in you. He's just not interested in marriage and kids.

17–27: The not-marrying man.

Are you out of your mind—this guy is telling you in no uncertain terms that he's not up for it. *He told you he doesn't want kids.* When a guy tells you he doesn't want kids, that translates roughly as "I don't want kids!" Wake up. Pack up. Move on. There's nothing worse than living with the idea that you may have persuaded someone into doing something they're not interested in. Aren't you going to wonder how things might have been different? Aren't you going to worry the marriage is a sham? Aren't you going to raise the kids alone?

> ***Question exception:** If he won't come over to kill a roach, subtract 5 points! What do you think we keep them around for?

Chapter 12 score: _____

Cumulative score: _____

Getting the Last Word In

How do you know when you find the No-Bullshit Guy?

Penelope had just returned from a trip with her father when she got a phone call informing her of her uncle's death. Although he had not been well months earlier, she had spoken to him while on their trip and he was feeling good and joking around, so his sudden death was shocking. He had been her favorite uncle growing up, and she cared about him deeply. She was committed to a show that was part of a festival and there were no understudies, so she had to perform at eleven P.M. the night before his nine A.M. funeral. She didn't drive, and due to the infrequent buses available to his small town, as hard as she tried to work it out, it wasn't feasible for her to make the funeral. She mentioned to a friend of hers that she was saddened because she felt a lack of closure. He immediately suggested that he would take the day off from work, rent a car, pick her up and drive her to the funeral. Initially, she refused him. She felt it was too much to ask. But later, seeing no other way, she took him up on his offer. Not only did he pick her up at five A.M. at her apartment and drive for three hours, he accompanied her to the funeral, sat with her while she cried through the service—"Catholic and very aerobic"—met her "crazy" family, drove her to the burial, attended the gathering afterward, and then hurried her back for her show that evening. Not for nothing, but they're a couple now. She still talks about how she couldn't get over the fact that here was a guy, attending a funeral for someone he didn't even know, just to help her feel better. She found his selflessness extremely touching. This guy was willing to go out of his way for her when he got nothing out of it. Exactly.

That's the No-Bullshit Guy. That's the kind of guy you should marry.

Jack Bauer:
Ruining All Men for Women Forever

The following takes place between six and seven A.M. With the threat of nuclear attack hanging over his head, Jack Bauer chases down the mastermind behind the attack, wounds him, holds him over the side of a building to try to keep him from killing himself before he can determine the missile's location, finds a digital device that enables the air force to shoot down the missile, finds out his own government is going to turn him over to the Chinese government so he can be tried under their law for something he did to save the freaking world, and then fakes his own death. That took place in an hour. A single hour of the fourth day of Jack Bauer's life that we ladies have been lucky enough to be privy to. Want to know what Jack's accomplished on the other three days? Well, let's see . . . He foiled a political assassination one day. On another he stopped a different nuclear attack. And on the third day, he fought bioterrorism.

I know guys who can't reserve a rental car given four days. I know guys who wouldn't be able to figure out how to get a library card in four days. Guys who can't make a dinner reservation four days in advance. I used to think maybe I should date a rodeo rider, a police detective, a strong man in the circus—you know, a Real Man, a butch guy, who could take care of shit (me). Then Jack Bauer came along and showed me a world I never knew existed. Not only are his instincts always right on target—none of that tortured hemming and hawing over whether he should order the pork tenderloin or the filet mignon—but he can infiltrate the Chinese embassy, kidnap a Chinese research scientist who is working as a freelance operative for terrorists, get information out of the guy, and as if that's not enough, he can then take a moment to tell his girlfriend *HE LOVES HER AND HE WANTS TO SPEND THE REST OF HIS LIFE WITH HER.*

You can't pick up a phone and call me? Did you have to remove the batteries from you cell phone to avoid detection by passive triangulation? I didn't think so. So what's your excuse, you pussy?

In a calm moment, I'm able to concede that Jack Bauer is now for all intents and purposes dead. And he's also a fictional character. A character most likely created by some guys as insane wish fulfillment. But as he put on those aviator sunglasses and walked down that train track alone, I wondered to myself what will he do, now that he's "dead"? Where will he go? And in my heart of hearts, I hope he's coming to find me.

THE SCORE

We've been through a lot together, you and I, and now you're all grown up and ready to score guys on your own. Just remember, wherever you go, whoever you meet, I'll be there. I'm in the queasy feeling you get in the pit of your stomach when you examine his shoes for the first time. I'm in the champagne bubbles that tickle your nose at that surprise party he planned for you when you got your promotion. I'm singing show tunes at the bar with that gay guy. And that gay guy. And that gay guy. So get out there, and find that almost-perfect guy. Or stay right where you are, depending. Either way, I'm right there with you. But not in a creepy way.

650–909: Master and commander.
This guy is ready to take the voyage with you. The wind is in your sails, and adventure is out there just waiting for you. So set the main sail, and let him shiver your timbers! You found good booty.

435–649: Don't give up the ship!
This guy is worth fighting for, even if he occasionally springs a leak when you think it should be smooth sailing. You might have to engage in a little swordplay, but eventually you get what you want. Stand firm, me hardy, and you'll see solid ground yet.

295–434: Walk the plank.
Avast! You deserve someone better! I think it's time to tell someone buh-bye. Seriously, how many times does he have to mess up before you wrap a blindfold around his eyes, give him back his CDs, and send him on his way? Find a vessel that sails right.

294–349: Marooned.
You might as well be alone. Get a volleyball, slap a wig on it, and give it a name. It'll be just as good. Why are you hanging on to this guy? Because your fear of loneliness is worse than your low self-esteem? Better to spend $125 for fifty minutes a week with a professional than another second with this guy! If you need a little strength to go it alone, belly up to the bar, and have one on me.

Oh, one last thing

Most of the time my guy makes me feel:

  a Happy

  b Frustrated

  c Miserable

No matter how he scored, if you didn't answer (a) on this one, you've got some serious thinking to do. Nobody's perfect. My apologies to Halle Berry, but I hear even she's retouched. Your job isn't to find the perfect guy. It's to find the guy you can live with. And when you find that guy, you'll feel good when you're with him. Anything less will not do. If you find yourself with an endless string of "whys" constantly running through your head—Why isn't he calling? Why doesn't he feel the same way I do? Why does he spend so much time with my friend Christina?—step off the treadmill, my little hamster of love. No matter how good he looks on paper, how RIGHT he seemed when you met him, if you feel like shit, get out of it. Life is too short to be spent with a guy who wears elevator shoes. You never know—at the next poetry reading, the next indie rock show, the next volunteer project, the next kickboxing match, that "master and commander" just might show up. And you wouldn't want to miss him while taking another disappointing "I can't make it after all" cell phone call from a "marooned."

PS: What is up with your friend Christina? You may want to keep an eye on her. I think she's into your guy.

Allison Castillo is a New York City comedian and writer who has appeared on Comedy Central's *Premium Blend*, Paramount television's *The World Stands Up* and VH-1's *Best Week Ever*.